Friends for Dinner

FoodAidsPeople

aids
a ripple in
spirals out.

Food.   people.
cross and nourish.

attend to us
our lives are precious too.

—Elizabeth St. John

All proceeds from *Friends for Dinner*
benefit Meals on Wheels for People with AIDS.

ISBN 0-9630870-0-2   Copyright 1991 by Volunteers of America, Colorado branch. Printed in USA.

Table of Contents

"I'm not sure what I expected to find on the new Meals on Wheels routes for people with AIDS, but it wasn't Bob.

The first time I saw Bob, he was lying on a cot in a fleabag hotel across the street from the Capitol. His door was open a crack, letting the sounds of daytime television leak into the hall. When I knocked, he rolled over just enough to see who I was, then motioned toward a tiny, junk-covered table at the foot of his bed.

The hot lunch I had hurried upstairs with went on the table for now. Bob wasn't in the mood to eat. He felt like hiding in his room, overcome by the AIDS virus that was eating away at his body."

From "An Inside Look at AIDS" by Linda Castrone,
Rocky Mountain News.

Some people did not work today. Some didn't make love. Some did not die and some didn't pay taxes. But everybody ate. Everyone eats every day, if even, to evoke two extremes, a sandwich from a soup line or a can of Ultra Slim Fast. Eating is our common bond.

Most of us prepare our own meals, or buy them, or enjoy them cooked for us, at a restaurant, say, or a friend's home. We seldom eat alone.

But some people do eat alone and some are so alone, without families or friends, and sometimes so weak and tired that they cannot feed themselves.

In Denver, the Volunteers of America Meals on Wheels for People with AIDS Program delivers fresh, well balanced, nutritious meals to over sixty people a day, people with AIDS or AIDS-related conditions who can no longer shop for and prepare their own food. This program nourishes the bodies and spirits of those who receive meals, helping them maintain as independent a life as possible, while providing them with daily human contact.

This program responds to all who call on it and so the program is itself in constant need of help.

This cookbook is published to benefit Volunteers of America Meals on Wheels for People with AIDS. Everyone who has worked on this project has generously donated their time and energy; including Madeleine St. John and her seemingly endless number of offspring who have edited the text, tested the recipes and illustrated the cover, and the chefs whose menus and recipes you have here. All the proceeds feed people.

If you would like more information on Volunteers of Americas Meals on Wheels for People with AIDS program or would like to volunteer as a VOA meal driver, please call 303-297-2136.

Bill St. John
November, 1991
Wine writer and dining critic for the
Rocky Mountain News.

Acknowledgement

This cookbook is a family affair. The inspiration to write it came after I visited my daughter, Anne, in San Francisco. Anne is a volunteer there with Project Open Hand. She delivers meals to people with AIDS and AIDS-related conditions who are unable to cook for themselves.

I wanted to help the people of Denver who are themselves finding ways to live with this disease. *Friends for Dinner* was born. All the proceeds from the book's sale go to Volunteers of America's Meals on Wheels for People with AIDS Program.

For help with the book, I am deeply grateful most especially to the members of my family: To my husband, Bill, for his constant support and encouragement. To Elizabeth, for the illustration and poem for the book cover. To Bill, for his expert advice in the choice of wines to complement each menu. To Robert, for the many hours spent editing my interviews. And to Paul, my sous-chef, for testing and tasting many of the recipes.

A special note of thanks goes to all the twenty-eight chefs who are featured in this book. Meeting and interviewing them was a fascinating experience. I came away from my visits with them convinced that, although their culinary styles range widely, they all share a passion for food, a strong creative drive and a common devotion to their craft. I also wish to thank the members of the *Friends for Dinner* committee: Celeste Clark, Gail Pitts, Edie Acsell, Joan Cotton, Marge Cozart, Clare Liem and Michael James who all shared their talents and were always there when I needed help.

Thank you to the students and friends of my cooking school for help testing the recipes. Thank you to Monique Davis for the design and layout of the book.

I also want to thank, in advance, all who will help introduce this book and bring many "friends for dinner."

Madeleine St. John
August, 1991

Wouldn't it be nice if a well-known chef could write your dinner party menu, with recipes and wine selections?

Well, that's what this book is, a compilation of the menus that twenty-eight different Colorado chefs would cook if they were to invite "friends for dinner." Each menu is a complete dinner, but individual items and recipes from one chef's menu can easily be combined with the recipes of another chef. You be the judge. The index lists all the recipes by category.

You can get to know these Colorado chefs a bit by reading the short introductions that precede each menu.

The wine suggestions accompanying each menu were added by Bill St. John, wine writer and dining critic for *Rocky Mountain News*. The wine suggestions are merely guidelines. If you cannot find the identical wine, the exact vintage or producer, substitute a similar type of wine. St. John's suggestions indicate the types of wines that would best accompany individual menu items. "Wine and food," he says, "go together just like people in pairs do. They're either alike in some way, they both like camping, say, or they complement each other's strength and weakness, sort of the Champagne taste and beer budget types."

Madeleine's Pantry supplements the menus in the book. It is a selection of basic recipes such as stocks and sauces that may be called for elsewhere in the book.

All the book's recipes have been tested by Madeleine St. John.

Chef George Atwell
The Broadmoor Hotel

The Broadmoor Hotel in Colorado Springs, one of America's premier resorts, has a colorful and renowned history. The pink palazzo at the foot of Cheyenne Mountain has been a retreat to the illustrious and famous. Ever since its opening on June 29, 1918, it has been a haven from the harried world.

The Broadmoor offers a myriad of activities including golfing, skiing, ice-skating, tennis and boating. One of its great attractions is its many fine restaurants. George Atwell, Executive Sous-Chef Tournant, who created the following menu for us, works closely with the Executive Chef in overseeing all the dining facilities, from the beautiful and romantic Charles Court Restaurant and the elegant Penrose Room to the ever - popular Tavern.

A graduate of the Culinary Institute in Hyde Park, New York, Chef Atwell credits his Italian grandmother for giving him his love of cooking. He fondly remembers the times he spent as a little boy in her kitchen watching her prepare pasta and the like. Upon graduation from the Culinary Institute, he went to Miami, Florida, where he was employed by the Hyatt Hotel. There he advanced his way to sous-chef and eventually was in charge of all its evening restaurants. He joined the Hyatt Regency in Los Angeles in 1984, and from there came to the Broadmoor in 1987, bringing along his wealth of expertise.

Menu for six to Eight

Sweet Corn, Black Bean and Artichoke Heart Salad with Basil Cumin Dressing

Medallions of Venison with Pear, Lingonberry, Apple Chutney

Chocolate Raspberry Won Ton

Wine Recommendations

Juve y Camps Brut Cava, San Sadurni de Noya

1990 Morgon, Louis Latour, Beaujolais

Bonny Doon Infusion of Framboise, Santa Cruz

"These are some of the recipes from our numerous food demonstrations at the Broadmoor. Some have a Southwest flair and others use ingredients from the fall season. The dessert is a creation that I serve in Charles Court that uses a Japanese won ton with a French dessert filling."
—George Atwell

Sweet Corn, Black Bean and Artichoke
Heart Salad with Basil Cumin Dressing

Serves 6 to 8

Salad

1/2 cup bacon, cut in julienne

1/2 medium size red onion, diced

1/2 red bell pepper, diced

1 cup fresh sweet corn, cooked

1/2 cup black beans, cooked

12 artichoke hearts

6-8 radicchio leaf cups

Basil Cumin Dressing
Yield: about 2 cups

1 Tbsp. shallots, minced

1/2 tsp. garlic, minced

2 Tbsp. fresh basil, chopped

3/4 tsp. ground cumin

1/2 tsp. ground black pepper

1/2 cup balsamic vinegar

1 1/4 cups olive oil

Salt to taste

Fry bacon until crisp. Remove bacon. Drain excess grease. Add onions and sauté until limp. Add peppers, corn, black beans and bacon. Toss until warm. Transfer to a bowl. Add the artichoke hearts and toss.

Combine dressing ingredients. Add enough dressing to moisten salad ingredients. Let marinate overnight. (Leftover dressing will keep for several days in the refrigerator.)

Presentation: Place a radicchio leaf cup on a cold salad plate. Spoon a cup of salad over it.

Medallions of Venison with Pear, Lingonberry, Apple Chutney

Serves 6 to 8

Allow two venison medallions, 3/4 inch thick, per person
  (This recipe can also be prepared with medallions of pork.)

Pear, Lingonberry, Apple Chutney

2 cups apple juice

1/2 cup cider vinegar

1/4 cup brown sugar

1 tsp. fresh thyme, chopped

2 Tbsp. fresh mint, chopped

1 tsp. green
  peppercorns, crushed

2 Tbsp. butter

1 pear, peeled, cored and diced

1 Red Delicious apple, peeled,
  cored and diced

1/4 cup lingonberry preserves
  (may use red currant jelly
  or whole cherry jam)

1 tsp. fresh mint, chopped

1 tsp. fresh thyme, chopped

In a saucepan over medium-high heat, combine apple juice, vinegar, brown sugar, 1 tsp. thyme, 2 Tbsp. mint and green peppercorns. Cook for a few minutes until sugar is dissolved, stirring occasionally. Continue cooking until mixture becomes syrupy, about twenty minutes.

Meanwhile, in a sauté pan melt the butter and sauté the apple and pear for two to three minutes. Add to the syrup mixture and mix. Lower heat to simmer. Add lingonberry preserves and a teaspoon each of fresh mint and thyme. Mix well. Remove from the heat and let cool.

Sauté medallions in a little melted butter for two to three minutes on each side. Serve hot with chutney on top.

Serves 6 to 8

Chocolate Ganache
Yield: 12 ounces

10 ounces semi-sweet chocolate

1 cup heavy cream

2 Tbsp. Chambord liqueur

In a double boiler over simmering water, melt the semi-sweet chocolate with the heavy cream. Remove from heat when it is three-quarters melted and work it with a spatula until it has completely dissolved. Add Chambord liqueur. Let mixture cool until thickened.

Won Tons

1 package won ton wrappers (2 inches by 2 inches)

1 egg, beaten

12 ounces chocolate ganache

1 pint fresh raspberries

1/2 cup raspberry jam

1 cup peanut oil

Brush each won ton wrapper with egg wash (beaten egg). Pour 1/2 tablespoon of chocolate ganache over each won ton and place 4 raspberries and 1/4 teaspoon raspberry jam over it. Fold corner to corner and seal. Continue until mixture is used up. (The won tons may be frozen at this point. Do not thaw before frying.)

When ready to use, heat 1 cup peanut oil in a heavy sauté pan. Be sure the oil is very hot. Fry 3 to 4 won tons at a time for 2 to 3 minutes or until crisp.

1 pint vanilla ice cream

1/2 cup chocolate sauce (Hershey's)

1/4 cup powdered sugar

Presentation: Place a scoop of vanilla ice cream in a coupe glass with 3 to 4 won tons. Drizzle with chocolate sauce. Dust with powdered sugar.

Chef Rebecca Benchouaf
Tuscany

In speaking with American-born Chef Rebecca Benchouaf, one feels her unsurpassed enthusiasm for her profession. This love of cooking emerged during the several summers she worked in a French restaurant located in Lake City, a small resort town in Southwest Colorado. It was there, under the guidance of a European-trained and very disciplined French chef, with an extraordinary passion for food, that she began her career.

Rebecca chose not to pursue formal culinary training, but rather to apprentice in different restaurants to learn from a rich variety of chefs. On the advice of friends, she spent two and one-half years working in the Napa Valley in California.

Upon her return to Colorado, she became the executive chef of Lincoln One Hundred, where she was given freedom to experiment with many different cuisines and change the menu regularly. This in turn has enabled her to develop her own style of fresh, uncomplicated but refined cooking. In June of 1991 she became executive sous-chef at Tuscany, the restaurant for Loews Georgio Hotel. She is working with executive chef Tim Fields who was featured on the cover of the magazine, **Culinary Trend**. *The food at Tuscany is "Italian soul food" with emphasis on fresh ingredients.*

The following statement, an introduction to her menu for the cookbook, best exemplifies the philosophy of this young chef: "I love to cook good food, and by working in the restaurant, I have the opportunity to indulge in a passion and have others appreciate it. But, when I'm cooking for my family and friends, which is not as often as I like, I do it with certain things in mind. First of all, it must be nutritious, encompassing specific food groups. Secondly, it must be simple to prepare because my schedule doesn't allow much time. And, most important, it must taste good without being expensive. Some of my favorite flavors are those from my husband's native country of Morocco. One of the wonderful things about preparing food from other cultures is that it gives us a chance to explore other facets of the culture while breaking bread. Sharing food with family and friends is a universal gesture, and, with that in mind, please ENJOY!"

Menu For Six

Gamila: Moroccan Chicken Stew

Roasted Pepper and Tomato Salad

Ajina: Moroccan Flat Bread

Mint Tea and Cookies

Wine Recommendation

1989 Fleur de Carneros Pinot Noir, Carneros Creek

"To complete this meal, it is appropriate to serve mint tea. The Moroccan favorite is peppermint with lots of sugar. You can buy any kind of cookies you like or make them if you have the time. Sesame and honey or any nut cookies are a nice finishing touch. I prefer coconut macaroons."
—Rebecca Benchouaf

Serves 6

3 1/2 to 4 lbs. chicken legs or thighs, skinned
(The stew may also be prepared with 6
half chicken breasts, skinned and boned.)

1 medium onion, chopped

2 medium tomatoes, skinned and diced

1/2 bunch fresh cilantro, chopped

1 clove fresh garlic, minced

1/4 cup extra virgin olive oil

1/4 tsp. cayenne pepper

1/2 tsp. salt

1 Tbsp. paprika

1/4 Tbsp. turmeric

1 1/2 to 2 quarts water

4 large potatoes, peeled and cut in 1-inch cubes

1 small jar of Spanish olives

In a large pot, combine chicken legs or thighs, onion, tomatoes, cilantro, garlic, olive oil and spices. Cook over medium high heat, stirring occasionally, until the onions soften and the chicken begins to brown. Add water and simmer, partially covered, for 30 minutes. Add potatoes, carrots and more water if necessary. Continue to simmer until the potatoes and carrots are tender, about 30 minutes more.

Meanwhile, soak olives in 1 cup water for 20 minutes. Drain and add to the Moroccan Chicken Stew. Adjust seasoning with salt and cayenne pepper if a spicier stew is desired.

According to the Moroccan custom, everyone gathers around a low table and shares from one plate.

Roasted Pepper and Tomato Salad

Serves 6

3 bell peppers (any color)

3 large tomatoes, skinned

6 lettuce leaves

Preheat oven to 400°. Rub bell peppers and tomatoes with olive oil and salt. Place in a baking dish and bake until they begin to turn brown and the pepper skins can easily be removed, about 45 minutes. Cool. Remove the skins and seeds and chop coarsely. Add to vinaigrette.

Vinaigrette

2 Tbsp. white wine vinegar

8 Tbsp. olive oil

Salt and freshly ground pepper to taste

Pour white wine vinegar and olive oil into a jar with a tight-fitting lid. Shake well. Adjust seasoning with salt and pepper.

Ajina: Moroccan Flat Bread

Makes 16 4-inch circles

4 cups all purpose flour, sifted
3/4 to 1 cup lukewarm water
1/2 tsp. salt
2 Tbsp. butter, melted
2 Tbsp. peanut oil

Sift flour again with the salt. Place on a clean surface and make a well in the center. Pour half the lukewarm water into the well and begin to mix with your fingertips. Continue adding more water as you mix until a supple dough is formed. Knead for 10 minutes and allow dough to rest, covered, in a warm place for 30 minutes.

Work with half the dough at a time, keeping the remaining dough covered. Roll each half of the dough in a cylindrical shape about 2 1/2 inches in diameter and slice into 1/4 -inch slices.

Roll out each slice on a floured surface to a very thin circle, about 4 inches in diameter. Brush each circle with melted butter and place two circles together, buttered sides in. Roll once again to press them together. They are now ready for frying.

Pour the peanut oil in a skillet and heat over medium heat. Cook the "tortillas" 5 minutes on each side. Stack on top of each other to keep warm. Serve warm.

Fred Bramhall and Mary Clark
The Bluepoint Restaurant

Overseeing the kitchen of the Bluepoint Restaurant is the talented husband-and-wife team of Fred Bramhall and Mary Clark. Their love for and dedication to fine cuisine has placed them among the rising stars of chefs of Colorado.

Fred has always enjoyed food preparation and credits his parents with giving him an appreciation of the art of cooking. Following his graduation from the Culinary Institute in Hyde Park, New York, he worked in several restaurants in Denver, spending seven years at Dudleys and then Chives American Bistro, where he said he "grew up as a chef."

Mary was a design student at the University of Colorado in Boulder where, just by chance, she became interested in cooking and soon discovered that she loved to do that best. She enrolled in classes offered by the well-known food writer and teacher, Lynne Kasper. Mary was the chef at the opening of Brendle's Restaurant, considered to be the first restaurant in Denver to offer "New American Cuisine." From there she went to Tante Louise, where she worked several years and made her mark as a chef.

Several years ago, Fred and Mary joined their multiple talents to open Bluepoint Catering. This led to the Bluepoint Restaurant and not long ago to the creation of their successful third venture, the Bluepoint Bakery.

A Late Summer Menu for Six

Wild Rice Waffle with Wild Mushroom Ragout

**Grilled Lamb with Mango Salad and Ginger
Jalapeño Vinaigrette**

Tarte Frangipane

Wine Recommendations

1989 Macon-Villages, Kermit Lynch Selection

1988 Zinfandel, Geyserville, Ridge Vineyards

*1989 Bassermann-Jordan Deidesheimer Langenmorgen Riesling
Spatlese, Rheinpfalz*

"This is inspired simply from the products that are available and at the peak of flavor during the harvest season. It is the kind of menu that we might prepare after spending the day in the Colorado mountains hunting mushrooms (at times even successfully!). Bon Appétit!"
—Fred Bramhall and Mary Clark

Serves 6 to 8

Wild Rice Waffle

3/4 cup raw wild rice
Pinch of salt
1 cup cake flour
1 tsp. baking powder
1/4 tsp. salt
Pinch of pepper
Pinch of nutmeg
3/4 cup sour cream
1/2 cup milk
2 eggs, separated
3 Tbsp. scallions, chopped
3 Tbsp. butter

Place 3/4 cup wild rice in a heavy saucepan with a pinch of salt and 4 cups water. Bring to a boil; simmer covered, until kernels are open and tender but not mushy (45 to 55 minutes). Drain excess liquid, cool.

Sift flour, baking powder, salt, pepper and nutmeg together. Combine sour cream, milk and egg yolks. Sauté scallions in butter until translucent, about 3 to 4 minutes. Cool briefly and add to sour cream mixture. Combine wet and dry ingredients. Add rice. Whip egg whites to medium stiff peaks and fold into batter.

Preheat Belgian waffle iron until very hot and spread batter to edges for a uniform waffle (not too much batter). Bake until crisp and quite brown, using the manufacturer's directions. The waffles can be made a day ahead, cooled, wrapped and reheated in a hot oven up to a day later.

Wild Mushroom Ragout
Yield: 2 cups

1 1/2 lbs. mushrooms, sliced (a combination of
      chanterelles, cepes, shitakes, oyster mushrooms
      or any wild or cultivated mushrooms)
3 shallots, minced
3 Tbsp. olive oil
1/4 cup dry white wine
1/4 cup chicken stock
1 1/4 cups cream
Salt and pepper to taste
1 Tbsp. fresh chives, minced

In a large saucepan, sauté mushrooms and shallots in olive oil for a few minutes. Cover and sweat until mushrooms give off their juices, about 10 minutes. Stir occasionally. Add white wine and simmer briefly. Add stock and cream; bring to a simmer and reduce until thickened, approximately 10 to 12 minutes. Do not let the mixture boil over. Season to taste with salt and pepper and stir in fresh chives.

This can be made well in advance, cooled and reheated in a double boiler.

Presentation: Reheat waffles in a 375°F oven for 6 to 8 minutes. Top each waffle with a large spoonful of mushroom ragout.

Grilled Lamb with Mango Salad and
Ginger Jalapeño Vinaigrette

Serves 6 to 8

1 to 1 1/2 lbs. tenderloin of lamb (room temperature)

Heat broiler or grill. Brush lamb with olive oil. Season with salt and pepper. Grill lamb until medium rare, about 5 minutes on either side. Let cool. Slice into thin slices and serve warm with the Mango Salad and Ginger Jalapeño Vinaigrette dressing.

Mango Salad

6 cups lettuce, cut or torn into bite-size pieces
    (use a mixture of interesting greens)
10 radishes, thinly sliced
1 red onion, thinly sliced
1 English cucumber, thinly sliced
2 mangoes, peeled and sliced
1/2 cup unsalted peanuts, toasted and chopped

Ginger Jalapeño Vinaigrette

3/4 cup olive oil, preferably extra virgin
1/4 cup rice wine vinegar
1 Tbsp. soy sauce
1 inch piece ginger root, peeled and minced
2 jalapeño peppers, seeded and thinly sliced
Salt and pepper to taste

Combine olive oil, rice wine vinegar, soy sauce, ginger and jalapeños in a jar and shake well. Season with salt and pepper.

Toss the dressing with the lettuce, radishes, red onions and cucumbers using just enough to moisten the salad without making it soggy.

Presentation: Divide the salad among 6 plates. Arrange lamb and mango slices on top of salad and sprinkle with peanuts.

This recipe invites variations: different oils or vinegars, add snow peas, subtract red onions, substitute papaya or plums for the mangoes.

Tarte Frangipane

Makes 1 9-inch tart

Filling

7 to 8 oz. almond paste
1/2 cup plus 3 Tbsp. sugar
1 stick (4 ounces) unsalted butter, at room temperature
3 eggs
3/4 cup cake flour, sifted
1/2 pint raspberries
Unbaked Sugar Crust Shell (recipe follows)
1/4 cup sliced almonds for garnish
Apricot preserves for glaze

Preheat oven to 350°F.

In the bowl of a processor fitted with the steel blade, cream the almond paste and sugar together until smooth. Add butter and finish creaming, scraping the bowl as necessary. Add eggs, one at a time, mixing well after each addition. Add cake flour and pulse until just combined. Do not overmix the ingredients.

Place an even layer of raspberries in the bottom of the unbaked sugar crust shell. Pour filling over raspberries covering them completely. Sprinkle with the sliced almonds and bake for 45 to 50 minutes. The tart is done when the top is slightly domed and the filling is firm in the center. Brush with melted apricot glaze made with apricot preserves, strained to remove the pulp.

Serve at room temperature, with or without cream or ice cream.

Sugar Crust Shell

1 stick (4 ounces) unsalted butter, cold
1/2 cup sugar
1 egg, slightly beaten
1 3/4 cups flour, sifted

In the bowl of a processor fitted with the steel blade, cream together the cold butter, cut into tablespoon-sized pieces and the sugar. Add egg and mix well. Add flour and pulse enough to combine. Do not overmix. Gather dough in a ball and wrap in waxed paper. Refrigerate 1/2 hour.

Flour top of dough lightly and roll to an 11-inch circle of 1/4-inch thickness. Transfer dough to a 9-inch fluted tart pan with removable bottom. Gently press it into the pan, fitting it snugly around the bottom edge and against the sides of the pan. Trim dough even with top of tart pan. Prick the bottom of the shell with a fork. Cover the crust loosely and chill until ready to use.

Executive Chef Odran Campbell
Augusta

The Westin Hotel at Tabor Center – She is the picture of elegance, serenity and beauty. Peach-colored linen combines with black-accented decor and large windows provide a sweeping view of downtown Denver. Augusta, the darling of the Westin Hotel at Tabor Center, has been satisfying the taste of a discriminating clientele for the last six years.

Recently, Augusta received a rare Four Diamond Award from the American Automobile Association and first place in the Always Buy Colorado Restaurant Contest. This award, given by the Governor, is an effort to build awareness of the high quality and variety of Colorado's agricultural products. Restaurants are judged on the variety of Colorado products used, the innovativeness of their use, the length of their promotion and the creativity of their promotional literature.

Presiding over the kitchen is Irish-born Executive Chef Odran Campbell. A desire to travel influenced Odran's choice of career. He attended a culinary school in Northern Ireland for three years, followed by a two-year study at Westminster College in London to acquire his City and Guild diploma, a prestigious English certificate. During this time he completed an apprenticeship at the world-renowned Savoy Hotel.

Odran then went to Canada, where he worked as chef in several hotels, ending up at the well-known Four Seasons in Toronto. From there his next destination was South Korea, where he spent three years working in

31

a hotel for a Japanese company. The Westin Hotel in Poussin, located in the southern tip of Korea, hired him as chef. He stayed there for another two years. An offer in 1986 to become executive sous-chef at the Westin Hotel in Dallas brought Odran to the United States. Five years later, he joined the Westin Hotel in Denver as their Executive Chef.

Chef Campbell characterizes his cuisine at Augusta as "New American," one which eschews the traditionally heavy European sauces, and uses as many Colorado products as possible. He says that he likes to "make the food, fun, interesting, lighter, colorful and enjoyable."

Menu for Six

Feuilleté of Salmon

Baked Chicken Breast with Forest Mushrooms

Grand Marnier Soufflé with Crème Anglaise

Wine Recommendations

1989 Pernand-Vergelesses Blanc, Antonin Guyon

1988 Pinot Noir, Winery Lake, Sterling Vineyards, Napa

"The menu featured above reflects the creative, elegant fare which is served at Augusta. It is designed with some of today's popular items."
—Odran Campbell

Serves 6

A sheet of puff pastry (12 inches x 12 inches, 3/8 inch thick)

1 egg wash (1 large egg yolk mixed with 2 tsp. water)

18 asparagus spears, blanched

1 Tbsp. butter

1 shallot, minced

3 peppercorns, crushed

1/3 cup Champagne

3/4 cup heavy cream

Salt and pepper to taste

1 large salmon fillet, skinned

1/4 cup salmon caviar, for garnish

Preheat oven to 425°F.

Roll puff pastry (your own or store-bought) into a square 12 inches x 12 inches, 3/8-inch thick, on a floured surface. Cut 6 4-inch x 4-inch squares. Invert the squares onto a moistened baking sheet and brush the tops with the egg wash, being careful not to let any of it drip down the sides. Chill the squares for approximately 15 minutes. Brush them again with the egg wash.

Bake the squares in the upper third of the oven for 10 minutes, reduce heat to moderately hot (375°F) and bake the squares for 10 minutes more, or until they are puffed and golden. Transfer pastries to a rack and let them cool. Cut off the top third of each pastry with a serrated knife to make a lid and scoop out the uncooked dough with a fork. Set aside.

Clean asparagus well and tie in bundles. Cook in boiling salted water until just crisp-tender. Drain.

Prepare sauce:

Heat 1 Tbsp. butter in a small pan over moderate heat. Sauté shallots until soft. Add crushed peppercorns and 1/3 cup Champagne and reduce to 2 Tbsp. Add heavy cream and continue cooking until reduced by 1/3. Season with salt and pepper.

Preheat broiler and oil broiler rack. Broil salmon 3-4 minutes on each side. Do not overcook. Cut 6 equal pieces to fit puff pastry squares.

Presentation: Fan 3 asparagus spears on each plate. Place 1 piece of salmon between each puff pastry square. Nap sauce over and garnish with some salmon caviar on the side. Serve immediately.

Baked Chicken Breast with Forest Mushrooms

Serves 6

7 chicken breast halves, boned and skinned

1 egg

1/4 cup heavy cream

1 Tbsp. butter

1 small shallot, minced

1 clove garlic, minced

2 Tbsp. fresh herbs (mixture of basil, tarragon and chives)

4 Tbsp. shitake mushrooms, chopped

2 Tbsp. oyster mushrooms, chopped

3 Tbsp. parsley, minced

Preheat oven to 350°F.

Process 1 half chicken breast in a food processor fitted with steel blade. Slowly incorporate egg and heavy cream and continue processing, scraping sides of bowl occasionally, until smooth. Remove from processor and place in a small bowl. Cover and refrigerate for 1/2 hour.

Heat butter in small pan over moderate heat. Sauté shallot, garlic and herbs, stirring for 1 minute. Add mushrooms and cook, stirring occasionally, for 5 minutes. Set aside and chill. When chilled, add mushroom mixture to chicken mousse and mix well.

Make a small cut into center of each remaining chicken breast half and fill with some mousse, being careful not to tear the chicken. Place in greased flat baking dish. Bake, covered, for 30 minutes or until done. Serve garnished with minced parsley.

A combination of wild and brown rice goes well with this as a side dish.

Serves 6 to 7

Soufflé

1 Tbsp. butter, softened

2 Tbsp. sugar

1/4 cup butter

1/4 cup flour

1 cup milk

1 Tbsp. grated orange zest

4 egg yolks

4 egg whites

1/4 cup sugar

3 Tbsp. Grand Marnier

Preheat oven to 400°F.

Prepare 6 to 7 soufflé cups, 3/4 cup (6 ounces) each, by brushing with soft butter and tossing with sugar to coat inside of cup. Tap out excess sugar. Refrigerate soufflé cups until ready to use. (This step will help the soufflé to rise straight up.)

In a small bowl of an electric mixer, cream the butter and flour until smooth. Bring milk to a boil and slowly add to flour mixture, stirring. Transfer to a small saucepan and cook, stirring constantly, for 1 minute over moderate heat, to form a thick paste or roux.

Return roux mixture to bowl of an electric mixer and cool roux on slow speed. When paste has cooled to warm, add grated orange zest and egg yolks and continue to mix on slow speed for 2 minutes.

In another bowl with an electric mixer, beat egg whites until frothy and slowly add 1/4 cup sugar. Continue beating until stiff.

Add Grand Marnier to the roux base and mix until smooth. Lightly fold in beaten egg whites. Fill soufflé cups full.

Place soufflé cups on a baking sheet and bake for 17 to 20 minutes, until risen and brown on top.

Serve immediately with Crème Anglaise.

Crème Anglaise
Makes 1 1/2 cups

3 egg yolks
3 Tbsp. sugar
3/4 cup milk
1/2 cup half-and-half
1/4 cup heavy cream
3/4 tsp. vanilla
1 Tbsp. Grand Marnier

In small bowl of an electric mixer, combine egg yolks and sugar and beat for 1 minute.

Scald milk, half-and-half and heavy cream. Slowly pour hot milk mixture over egg yolk mixture.

Place all ingredients back on low heat and continue cooking, stirring constantly, until mixture coats the back of a spoon. (Do not let it boil.)

Place pan over a bowl of ice to stop cooking process. Cool, stirring occasionally and strain. Add vanilla and Grand Marnier. Refrigerate, covered, for several hours or overnight.

Richard Chamberlain
The Restaurant at the Little Nell

Richard Chamberlain's entrance into the culinary world may be unique. As a sophomore in high school, he decided to take a home economics class for no other reason than that he liked a girl in the class. Once in the course he was required to cook, something in which he had absolutely no interest. However, when he actually began to put ingredients together, he enjoyed it so much that he began to prepare meals for his family every night after basketball or football practice. He bought as many cookbooks as he could and experimented. By his senior year, Richard was quite proficient at his hobby and decided to make it his career.

He enrolled at a culinary college in Dallas, going to school during the day and working as an apprentice at night at the renowned restaurant The Mansion on Turtle Creek. All the chefs were French, very regimented and strict. It was difficult for Richard, young and new to the business, to understand this management mentality. Richard still remembers the humiliation he felt when a French sous-chef asked him to chop a big container of garlic. He started to do it with a knife, as he had learned at school, when the sous-chef approached him and yelled, "What are you doing? We did it that way twenty years ago." He then proceeded to grab the garlic, put it into the food processor and chop it in a few seconds.

After three years, he and another chef from The Mansion opened a restaurant in Dallas. Then he accepted a position as sous-chef with the

Bel-Air Hotel in Los Angeles. A call to be chef at a new Dallas restaurant, San Simeon, brought him back to his hometown. The restaurant became very successful and received national acclaim.

But on a trip to Aspen to attend the Aspen/Snowmass Food & Wine Classic in the summer of 1988, he met the manager of the Little Nell Hotel. The ninety-two room, luxury hotel was near completion and in need of a chef. Richard had fallen in love with the beauty of the area, so he became chef of the Restaurant at the Little Nell. He has held that post since the Restaurant opened in November, 1989.

Because the Hotel caters to skiers in the winter and hikers in the summer - all with very good appetites - the management asked him to create a cuisine that would be healthy and hearty, yet light. Since Aspen was far from any coast, he rejected Mediterranean cuisine and bypassed Italian or eclectic cuisine as too trendy. Instead he turned to the history of the town. Many people who migrated to Aspen were Europeans from Switzerland, the Alsace region of France and Austria.

To create a special cuisine for the restaurant, he combined the European techniques of curing, smoking and preserving, using natural ingredients of Colorado - wild game, fish, fruits and vegetables. He also discovered that the dryness of the mountain air required different cooking methods, such as braising instead of roasting. The final result is a hearty, healthy type of food which he calls "American-Alpine Cuisine".

This innovative chef has gone a step further to americanize the cuisine to suit his preferences and those of his clientele: the sauces forego heavy cream and are of clear, light reduction; the sausages are made with chicken with flavorings and pheasant with dried fruits, instead of pork and fat in the European tradition.

Bon Appétit magazine has labeled Chamberlain an "innovator." Dining at the elegant The Restaurant at the Little Nell is a feast for the eyes as well as the palate. Each plate is a triumphant interplay of texture , color and taste.

Menu for six

Smoked Rainbow Trout, Apple and Pistachio Salad with Lemon
Mint Vinaigrette

Oven Roasted Salmon with Potato Basil Crust and Warm
Tomato Mint Chutney

Chocolate Mint Truffle Cake

Wine Recommendations

1989 Kenwood Sauvignon Blanc, Sonoma

1989 Ponzi Pinot Gris, Oregon

Quady Elysium Black Muscat

*"A delightful summer menu sure to please the most discriminating
palate."*   *—Richard Chamberlain*

Smoked Rainbow Trout, Apple and Pistachio Salad
with Lemon Mint Vinaigrette

Serves 8 to 10 as a first course, 6 as a luncheon entrée

Salad

2 8-ounce smoked trout fillets, cut into diamonds

1/3 cup pistachios, toasted

1 Granny Smith apple, julienned

1 Red Delicious apple, julienned

1 leek, julienned (white part only)

2 heads frisée lettuce, cut up

Toss salad ingredients together with vinaigrette and arrange on cold plates.

Lemon Mint Vinaigrette
Makes about 2 cups

1/4 cup water

1 egg yolk

1 Tbsp. lemon juice

1 Tbsp. grated lemon zest

3/4 Tbsp. fresh mint, chopped

1 tsp. honey

1 1/2 cups peanut oil

Salt and white pepper to taste

Place water, egg yolk, lemon juice, lemon zest, mint and honey in a blender. Blend on medium speed for 30 seconds. Slowly add peanut oil to form an emulsion. Season with salt and white pepper.

Toss salad ingredients together with vinaigrette to taste and arrange on cold plates.

Oven Roasted Salmon with Potato Basil Crust
and Warm Tomato Mint Chutney

Serves 6

Salmon

6 salmon fillets - 6 ounces each, skin removed

3 small Idaho potatoes, peeled

12 fresh basil leaves

4 tsp. lemon juice

1/4 cup clarified butter (see Madeleine's Pantry)

4 Tbsp. peanut oil

Salt and white pepper to taste

12 basil leaves for garnish

Shape potatoes into oval cylinders. Slice paper thin and discard end pieces.

Lay 2 leaves of fresh basil on each salmon fillet. Lay potato slices over the top of the basil to look like fish scales. Brush potato slices with lemon juice. Season with salt and white pepper. Chill for 15 minutes.

Preheat oven to 375°F.

In a large sauté pan over medium heat, warm 3 Tbsp. clarified butter. Sauté fillets, potato side up, until edges begin to brown (if salmon and potatoes separate, press back together). Remove from heat and drizzle remaining clarified butter over fillets. Place sauté pan in oven and cook, uncovered, until medium (4 minutes). Do not turn. Remove from oven.

Presentation: Spoon warm tomato chutney over each plate. Place salmon with potato crust on top. Garnish each serving with 2 leaves of fresh basil. Serve immediately.

Tomato Mint Chutney

2 Tbsp. peanut oil

2 Tbsp. shallots, minced

1/2 tsp. garlic, minced

3 Tbsp. red onion, minced

1 Tbsp. Champagne vinegar

1 tsp. honey

1/4 tsp. pickling spices

Pinch of ground cumin

1/2 tsp. fresh ginger, minced

2 cups tomatoes, peeled, seeded and diced

Salt and white pepper to taste

1 Tbsp. fresh mint, chopped

In a 2 quart saucepan, over medium heat, warm 2 Tbsp. peanut oil and sauté shallots, garlic and red onion, stirring, for 2 minutes. Add vinegar, honey, pickling spices and cumin. Mix and reduce until dry (be careful not to let it burn). Add ginger, tomatoes, salt and white pepper. Stir and simmer, uncovered, for 25 minutes. Correct seasoning and add fresh mint. Set aside. Serve warm.

Chocolate Mint Truffle Cake
(from pastry chef Michael Smith)

Serves 6 to 7

3/4 lb. semi-sweet chocolate

3/4 cup (1 1/2 sticks) unsalted butter

4 Tbsp. white crème-de-menthe

3/4 cup fresh mint leaves, packed

5 eggs, room temperature

Preheat oven to 375 F. Butter 6 to 7 ramekins, 3/4 cup (6 ounces) each, line bottom with parchment paper.

Cut chocolate in small pieces. Place with the butter in top of a double boiler over simmering water, stirring until melted and smooth.

While chocolate is melting, bring créme-de-menthe to a simmer in a small pan, add mint leaves, cover and remove pan form heat. Let stand 3 minutes. Press and strain the créme-de-menthe and mint leaf mixture. Add liquid to the chocolate-butter when completely melted. Set aside.

In a medium-sized bowl, whip eggs until light and thick, about 7 minutes. Transfer chocolate mixture to a large bowl. Fold 1/4 of the eggs into the chocolate mixture. Fold in the rest to the eggs.

Divide batter into ramekins. Place filled ramekins in a 9x12x2 inch pyrex dish. Pour hot water into the dish until the lower half of the ramekins are standing in water. Place pan in oven for 7 minutes. Remove from the oven and cover with foil. Return to the oven and cook for 20 minutes more. Remove from the water bath and chill for 2 hours.

When ready to serve, run a hot, wet knife around the side of each ramekin and invert on a plate. Serve with whipped cream.

Jim Cohen
Wildflower Inn, The Lodge at Vail

The Lodge at Vail was built in 1962 at the foot of America's largest ski mountain. It is a member of the Leading Hotels of the World and is owned by VSOE Associated Hotels, the company that runs the famous Venice Simplon Orient-Express Train. Jim Cohen is the executive chef for the Lodge.

"I always wanted to eat, " says Jim. "I worked on a road crew when I was nineteen years of age and the time I looked forward to the most was lunch-break."

While he was growing up, great emphasis was placed on family gatherings, especially during Jewish holidays which center around the table. "I loved cooking and always felt comfortable in the kitchen."

He started cooking professionally in 1974 in New York, in a restaurant called Mulligans, to help pay his tuition to the University of Buffalo.

Jim enrolled at the Culinary Institute of America in 1976. Upon graduation, he worked for a year at the Colony Square Hotel in Atlanta, spending half of the time in the Garde-Manger department of the kitchen and the other half as a general apprentice in a small French restaurant, the Gourmet Room.

After leaving the Colony Square, he and his wife, also a graduate of the Culinary Institute, decided to tour the country but ran out of money in Denver. She secured a position at Dudleys (now Chives) and he at the

Denver Country Club. A year later, Jim and a partner opened a catering business, The Plum Tree Caterers, and a restaurant, The Plum Tree Café. However, as Jim remarks, "Two chefs do not work well in the same kitchen." He left the partnership to become the chef at Tante Louise restaurant for three years.

From there, he came to Vail, where he has been the executive chef at the Lodge since 1983. His duties are to oversee its two restaurants, the Café Arlberg and the Wildflower Inn, which he opened in 1984. This most pleasant dining room is a Travel Holiday award-winning restaurant with an international wine list.

Despite its renown, the cuisine at the Wildflower Inn does not have a particular style. It reflects Italian, Jewish and California influences and most of the products come from the West Coast. One could say that the cuisine is mostly regional American, with an emphasis on freshness.

The Lodge at Vail holds many elaborate functions annually. One with which Jim has been closely involved for the past five years is the highly successful Gastronomique Affair, held every January. For this event, he brings in four chefs from different regions of the United States: the East and West Coasts, the Mid-West and the South. Each chef, including himself, is paired with a different winemaker. Each night brings the creations of a new chef with a different winemaker, and together they engage in classes and gourmet dining. A first in January, 1991, was the appearance of four women chefs: Diane Kennedy, Lydia Bastianich, Lidia Shires and Nancy Silverton.

This multi-talented chef had a change-of-pace in September, 1991, when he went to Europe to work in a hotel owned by VSOE Associated Hotels in Florence, Italy and then to Nice, France, where he is plying his skills in a small, ten-table restaurant.

Menu for Six

Lobster Cake with Tomato-Chive Butter Sauce

Lamb Shanks with Garlic Mashed Potatoes

Torta Regina

Wine Recommendations

1990 Sauvignon Blanc, Matanzas Creek, Sonoma

1985 Chateau Gruaud-Larose, St. Julien

Blandy's 10-year Old Malmsey Madeira

"This menu includes some of the most popular dishes done over the years. The lamb shank recipe dates back to my days at Tante Louise restaurant. It is a perfect winter menu. I picture people sitting by the fire around an old table, sipping wine and enjoying the meal."

–Jim Cohen

Lobster Cake with Tomato-Chive Butter Sauce

Serves 6

Lobster Cake

1/2 cup heavy cream

4 slices white bread, trimmed of crusts

1 1/2 cups cooked lobster meat, finely chopped

2 eggs, beaten

1 1/2 Tbsp. fresh lemon juice

Salt and pepper to taste

1 Tbsp. butter

1 Tbsp. peanut oil

Tomato-Chive Butter Sauce (recipe follows)

In a small saucepan, cook the cream over medium heat, stirring occasionally until the amount of cream is reduced by half. Cool.

Preheat oven to 400°F.

Tear the bread into pieces and purée in a food processor to make crumbs.

In a large bowl, combine the cream, bread crumbs, lobster meat, eggs, lemon juice, salt and pepper. Shape the mixture into 6 patties. Refrigerate for 20 minutes.

In a sauté pan or skillet, melt the butter with the oil and sauté the lobster patties until golden brown. Transfer the patties to a greased baking sheet and bake in the preheated oven for 5 to 7 minutes.

Presentation: Spoon 2 to 3 tablespoons of Tomato-Chive Butter Sauce with a sprinkling of chives on each of 6 warm plates and place a lobster cake on top. Serve immediately.

Tomato-Chive Butter Sauce

7 Roma tomatoes, peeled and coarsely chopped

1 bay leaf

5 peppercorns

1/2 shallot, diced

1 cup dry white wine

2 sticks (8 ounces) chilled butter, cut into tablespoons

1/2 cup chopped fresh chives

Purée the tomatoes in a blender or food processor. In a large saucepan, place the tomato purée, bay leaf, peppercorns, shallot, and white wine. Cook over medium-high heat until the mixture is reduced by three-fourths. Remove from heat. Add the cold butter to the tomato mixture a tablespoon at a time, whisking constantly. Strain through a sieve and keep warm in a double boiler over warm water until serving.

Serves 6

Lamb Shanks

6 1-pound lamb shanks

Salt and pepper to taste

5 Tbsp. flour

1/2 cup olive oil

1 onion, diced

1 carrot, peeled and diced

2 celery ribs, diced

1/2 fennel bulb, sliced

2 cups dry white wine

6 Tbsp. Dijon mustard

1 bay leaf

1 Tbsp. peppercorns

1 whole garlic bulb, unpeeled, cut in half

6 cups (1 1/2 quarts) chicken stock (see Madeleine's Pantry)

Preheat the oven to 350°F.

Season the lamb shanks with salt and pepper and dredge them in 2 Tbsp. of flour. In a sauté pan or skillet, heat half of the olive oil and sear the shanks, 2 or 3 at a time, until golden brown, adding olive oil as necessary. Transfer the shanks to a heavy ovenproof casserole with a lid, reserving the sauté pan or skillet and its juices.

In the sauté pan, place the onion, carrot, celery and fennel and sauté the vegetables until tender, about 8 to 10 minutes. Add the remaining 3 tablespoons of flour to the vegetables, mix well and continue cooking over medium-high heat, stirring constantly for 3 to 4 minutes. Add the white wine and stir. Bring to a boil and reduce the mixture by half. Add the mustard, bay leaf, peppercorns, garlic and stock and bring to a boil.

Pour the vegetable mixture over the shanks and bake, covered, in the preheated oven for about 2 hours, or until very tender, turning the shanks every 30 minutes.

Remove shanks from the pan and strain the liquid through a sieve, pressing the vegetables through with the back of a spoon. Place the liquid in a saucepan and cook over medium heat until it is thick enough to coat a spoon. Remove all the fat from the top. Adjust seasonings.

Presentation: Place a lamb shank with some garlic mashed potatoes on a warm plate. Spoon sauce over shank and potatoes.

Garlic Mashed Potatoes
Serves 6

6 cloves garlic, skin on
2 1/2 lbs. (3 large) potatoes, cubed
1 cup heavy cream
2 Tbsp. butter
Salt and pepper to taste

Roast garlic for 30 minutes in 350°F oven (see Madeleine's Pantry). Cool. Peel and mash. Cover potatoes with water and cook until tender. Drain. Heat cream and butter. Add garlic. Add to potatoes and mash with an electric mixer until smooth and fluffy. Season with salt and pepper to taste.

Serves 10

10 ounces semi-sweet chocolate, chopped coarsely

8 eggs, separated, room temperature

3/4 cup sugar

Grated zest of 1 orange

Grated zest of 1 lemon

1/4 cup each: pecans, walnuts, filberts
    and almonds, finely ground

Adjust oven rack to middle position. Preheat the oven to 350°F. Butter a 9 1/2-inch springform pan; line the bottom with waxed or parchment paper and butter it.

In the top of a double boiler over simmering water, melt the chocolate, stirring occasionally. When it has melted, set it aside to cool just until it is warm.

In a large bowl, beat the egg yolks with an electric mixer; beat in 1/2 of the sugar, a little at a time, until the mixture is thick and light in color (about 7 minutes). Add melted chocolate, grated zest of orange and lemon and ground nuts and beat the mixture until it is well combined.

In another bowl, beat the egg whites until they hold soft peaks. Beat in the remaining sugar, a little at a time, and continue beating until whites hold stiff, glossy peaks. Fold 1/4 of the whites into the chocolate mixture until well incorporated, then gently fold in the remaining whites.

Pour mixture into the prepared pan and bake for 45 to 50 minutes or until set. Cool completely on a cake rack.

Remove the pan sides and invert on a serving platter. Carefully remove the paper. Glaze with chocolate ganache. This cake freezes well.

Chocolate Ganache

1/2 cup cream
2 Tbsp. sugar
8 ounces semi-sweet chocolate, coarsely chopped

Warm cream and sugar together and stir until sugar is dissolved. Add chocolate and continue stirring until it is melted.

Glaze cake and refrigerate it for 30 minutes to set glaze. Remove it from the refrigerator to a cool place.

THAnk you for
Supporto the Most
Important issue.
of this Century
keep Coghtig
Mark L

Noel Cunningham
Strings

Noel Cunningham followed his family into the culinary world. His dad was a chef at the Gresham Hotel - Dublin's answer to London's Savoy Hotel - and his uncle was executive chef for all of Aer-Lingus operations at Dublin Airport, a prestigious position in the days when good food was an important part of the travel industry.

Noel was not especially fond of school, so when he turned fourteen, an age in Ireland when one is allowed to work, a family council convened to determine his future. It decided that he would go to work for his uncle. A tailor came to the house to take his measurements for his work uniform and in no time, he was launched on a new life. The working experience proved both good and bad. Good, because his uncle saw to it that he received the best possible training. Bad, because his uncle and the staff were especially demanding of him to prove that there was no favoritism.

After three and a half years, Noel moved to London where he was hired as an apprentice at the famous Savoy Hotel. At the same time, he enrolled at Westminster College to study for a City and Guilds, an important certificate and the English equivalent of a diploma for all types of businesses including culinary. For four years, he worked six days a week and went to school on his day off. But he loved this life of hard work and felt like "the luckiest person in the world."

Interestingly, the training his uncle had given him proved particularly helpful to him at the Savoy. During his apprenticeship in the butchery section, the butcher fell ill. A certain cut of veal was required and Noel, who knew exactly what to do, prepared it for the kitchen. The chef was most impressed with Noel's work.

Noel also proved a quick study, and by age twenty-three, was named sous-chef at the Savoy. He was the youngest ever to attain this rank, especially notable because he was Irish. In those days in England the best chefs were either French or Italian. The Hotel was very proud of him and would mention his accomplishments to its new recruits. Despite the fact that Noel was one of 125 cooks and the fourth in line to become a chef, he stayed at the Savoy for ten years.

In 1976, Noel and his family went to Los Angeles on vacation. He observed that the people looked very healthy and wondered if this part of the world would not be a better place to raise his little girls. He never returned to London. He resigned his position at the Savoy and took a job as sous-chef at Harry's Bar and American Grill in Century City, California, one of several restaurants owned and operated by the Spectrum Food Corporation. Noel advanced rapidly over the next few years and eventually became chef for all the Spectrum food holdings.

The late seventies were an exciting and revolutionary period in the California culinary field. Chefs like Jean Blanchet introduced and experimented with different ingredients and techniques of nouvelle cuisine. For Noel, it was also a time when he learned the financial side of the restaurant business.

From 1980 to 1986, he was chef at Beverly Hills' exclusive supper club, Touch. He was given "carte blanche" to do whatever he wanted with the best-equipped kitchen, the best staff - including a pastry chef and two sous-chefs he hired from the Savoy - and a first class menu. Touch was the top of the échelon for celebrities, with no fewer than thirty-six VIP tables on opening night. It was a club which saw the likes of Michael Caine, Marvin Davis, George Burns, Shirley Maclaine and Madonna.

"I learned a very valuable lesson there and one which has helped me in the restaurant business", Noel says. "No matter how important people are, each likes to know that someone truly cares about them."

Touch was sold in 1986. Toby Robertson, a former colleague from Spectrum Foods, persuaded Noel to come to Denver to consider opening a new restaurant on the site of the defunct Café Ronchetti. Noel loved the space. Strings opened on July 22nd of that year.

This upscale eatery, considered one of Denver's best restaurants, is the "in" spot for politicians, socialites and sports and media celebrities. One feels pampered in this pleasant oasis situated only minutes from downtown. The cuisine is "contemporary American cuisine" and uses the freshest of ingredients and a profusion of fresh herbs.

Noel is also proud of his new venture, Ciao! Baby, a contemporary Italian trattoria located in southeast Denver. His wife, Tammy, helps him supervise the two restaurants.

A profile of the chef would not be complete without mentioning another side of his nature and one beloved by Denverites: his complete dedication to helping people in need. The causes he actively supports are numerous and varied: Meals on Wheels for People with AIDS, Share Our Strength, Project Safeguard, and Sunshine House.

Noel's thoughtfulness is boundless. He wants every guest at Strings to have a memorable dining experience, from families with young children who are treated specially, to young people on prom night for whom he designs a reasonably-priced menu.

Menu for Four

Coho Salmon, Baby Mâche and Radicchio Salad with Orange
Vinaigrette

Penne Bagutta with Tomato Sauce

Charbroiled Eggplant and Champagne Vinaigrette

Italian Cream Cake

Wine Recommendations

1990 Sauvignon Blanc, Beaulieu Vineyard

1988 Chianti Rufina, Castello di Nipozzano, Frescobaldi

*"In the last ten years we have all become much more aware of the
devastating effects of AIDS in our society. We cannot ignore the issue any
more. If we all wait until it affects us personally, it will be too late.
Please read the information available and take time to educate your
children on the recommended preventative steps. Children are the most
precious thing we have. Please keep them safe."* —*Noel Cunningham*

Coho Salmon, Baby Mâche and Radicchio Salad
with Orange Vinaigrette

Serves 4

Salad

8 pieces baby mâche

7 leaves radicchio

1 small orange

1/2 cup red bell pepper, roasted, peeled and diced
   (see **Madeleine's Pantry**)

1/2 cup tomatoes, diced

1/2 cup enoki mushrooms

1 Coho salmon (3/4 to 1 lb.)

Salt and pepper to taste

2 Tbsp. olive oil

8 edible flowers

Heat broiler. Wash mâche and radicchio. Drain well. Julienne 3 leaves of radicchio. Peel orange and divide into segments. Cut each segment in half. Place mâche, julienned radicchio, bell pepper, tomatoes, orange segments and enoki mushrooms in a medium-size bowl. Set aside.

Sprinkle inside of Coho salmon with salt and pepper. Brush outside of fish generously with olive oil. Broil 3 to 4 minutes on each side or until done. Do not overcook.

Remove skin and bones from fish, slice into 1-inch strips, and set aside. Toss salad with Orange Vinaigrette (recipe follows).

Presentation: Place 1 radicchio leaf on each plate. Divide salad equally. Top with salmon strips. Decorate each plate with 2 edible flowers. Pass remaining vinaigrette.

Orange Vinaigrette
Makes about 1 1/2 cups

3 tsp. orange marmalade

6 Tbsp. orange juice

2 tsp. orange zest

4 Tbsp. rice vinegar

12 Tbsp. light olive oil

Dash of salt and pepper

Mix orange marmalade, orange juice, zest and rice vinegar in a small bowl. Slowly add light olive oil and blend well. Season with a dash of salt and pepper. Refrigerate until ready to use.

Serves 4

3 Tbsp. olive oil

2 chicken breast halves, deboned,
    skinned and cut in 1-inch strips

1 cup mushrooms, sliced

1 clove garlic, minced

15 crushed red pepper flakes

1/2 cup half and half

2 cups tomato sauce (recipe follows)

8 ounces fresh penne pasta or 4 ounces dried

1/3 cup freshly grated Parmesan cheese

12 fresh basil leaves, chopped

1/4 cup parsley, chopped

8 small broccoli florets, cooked

Heat oil in a heavy saucepan over medium heat. Add the chicken and sauté for 2 minutes, stirring occasionally. Add sliced mushrooms and sauté 1 more minute. Add minced garlic and crushed red pepper flakes. Mix well. Raise heat to medium-high. Add cream and reduce by half. Add tomato sauce. Bring to a boil, lower heat and simmer for 5 minutes.

In boiling salted water, cook penne until al dente. Drain well. Toss pasta with Tomato Sauce and sprinkle with Parmesan cheese, basil and parsley. Divide among 4 plates and surround with broccoli florets. Serve immediately while hot.

Tomato Sauce
Yield: 2 1/4 cups

1 1/2 Tbsp. olive oil

2 cloves garlic, minced

1 shallot, minced

1 16 ounce can whole tomatoes

3 fresh tomatoes, skinned, seeded and chopped

Heat oil in a medium-size pan over moderate heat. Add garlic and shallots and sauté, stirring until translucent. Add canned tomatoes and fresh tomatoes and mix well. Cook, uncovered, for 1/2 hour. Remove from heat and set aside until needed. (This sauce may be prepared ahead of time and reheated.)

Charbroiled Eggplant and Champagne Vinaigrette

Serves 4

Eggplant

1 eggplant
1/2 cup olive oil
Salt and pepper to taste
Pinch of garlic powder
4 small tomatoes, peeled, seeded and sliced
8 oz. buffalo mozzarella, diced

Slice eggplant in 8 slices. Brush both sides with olive oil. Season lightly with salt, pepper and a hint of garlic powder. Charbroil for 2 to 3 minutes on each side.

Presentation: Place warm eggplant on 4 plates with sliced tomatoes and buffalo mozzarella cheese. Pour Champagne Vinaigrette over all. Serve.

Champagne Vinaigrette
Makes 1 scant cup

2 Tbsp. Champagne vinegar
1/4 tsp. brown sugar
1/2 tsp. Dijon mustard
12 Tbsp. olive oil
1/4 tsp. lemon juice
Freshly ground black pepper
8 basil leaves, julienned

Mix Champagne vinegar, brown sugar and Dijon mustard together. Slowly add olive oil. When ready to use, add lemon juice, freshly ground black pepper and basil leaves. Mix well.

Italian Cream Cake

Serves 10 to 12

Cake

1 tsp. soda

1 cup buttermilk

2 cups all purpose flour

Pinch of salt

1 stick (4 ounces) unsalted butter, softened

1 stick (4 ounces) margarine, softened

1 1/2 cups granulated sugar

5 eggs, separated, room temperature

1 1/2 tsp. vanilla

1 cup pecans, ground

1 1/2 cups coconut

Cream Cheese Frosting (recipe follows)

Preheat oven to 350°F. Butter and flour 3 9-inch cake tins. Combine soda and buttermilk and let stand for 10 minutes. On a sheet of waxed paper, sift together the flour and salt.

In a bowl cream butter, margarine and sugar until light and fluffy. Add egg yolks, one at a time, beating well after each addition. Add vanilla. Add dry ingredients and buttermilk alternately to the butter mixture, beginning and ending with the flour. Beat egg whites until stiff. Fold into cake mixture. Add vanilla. Gently stir in 1 cup pecans and coconut. Divide the batter evenly into the cake tins and bake for 25 minutes. Do not overcook.

Cool one layer on a cake stand, the others on wire racks. Frost the bottom layer of the cake (the one on cake stand) with Cream Cheese Frosting. Set the second layer on top. Frost. Repeat with third layer. Frost entirely. Garnish with 1/2 cup ground pecans.

Cream Cheese Frosting

*Makes enough to fill and frost a
9-inch layer cake.*

1 8-ounce package cream cheese, softened

1 stick (4 ounces) unsalted butter, softened

1 tsp. vanilla

1 cup powdered sugar

1/2 cup pecans, ground, as garnish

*Using an electric mixer, combine cream cheese and butter in a mixing
bowl. Add vanilla and mix well. Gradually add sugar and beat until
frosting is of spreadable consistency.*

Christopher DeJohn
The Signature Room

Christopher DeJohn fondly remembers his Italian mother always in the kitchen cooking. That is the memory that fueled his desire to become a chef.

After high school and a year working in the food department of a hospital, he decided to enroll at the California Culinary Academy in San Francisco. However as Chris says, "You don't come out of school being a chef. The training and constant hard work that follow get you there."

Upon graduation from the Academy in 1978, he worked for awhile as a sous-chef for a large catering company in San Francisco at their restaurant on Market Street, the Orient Express.

From San Francisco, he moved down the coast to Carmel to take a job at Pebble Beach Country Club as an assistant banquet chef. The pay was not great but it was an excellent learning experience and it led to an appointment at the French restaurant, La Bohème. This establishment offered a fairly unusual restaurant concept: "One chef with a prix fixe menu and dinner only."

An acquaintance in Colorado contacted Chris to see if he would like to become chef of the restaurant at the Teller House in Central City during the opera season. He accepted the offer. He grew to love the work, the clientele and the Rocky Mountain area. When the opera season was over, he chose to make Colorado his home.

After several stints in different restaurants, he found a position with more flexible hours as a chef for King Soopers in its specialty meat department. What he enjoyed most about that job was dealing with the public, especially teaching his staff and customers how to cook. However, he missed the restaurant business and knew that he should return to it.

An opportunity presented itself four years ago when the position of chef became available at The Signature Room at Stapleton International Airport. His duties at the beginning consisted mainly of overseeing The Signature Room and the many banquets held there. Soon the restaurant's operating company, Concession Air, realized that his expertise would be valuable throughout the entire airport. Concession Air operates nineteen bars and snack-bars, four fast-food restaurants, and two full-service dining rooms. Chris now directs all of its food services, special functions and banquets. He initiates new concepts when needed, writes all the recipes and trains the cooks. Despite this vast scope of responsibility, Chris devotes twenty-five percent of his time to The Signature Room.

His interest in the culinary field extends beyond his work. Chris is active with Chefs de Cuisine, a group of chefs who meet once a month to exchange ideas. At present, he is training three apprentices who work at night through a program designed by Chefs de Cuisine.

Christopher DeJohn was one of several chefs nominated last year for the award "Best Chefs of Colorado".

Menu for Eight

Broiled Oysters Provencal

Imported Prosciutto Ham with Fresh Figs and Raspberries

**Colorado Tenderloin of Lamb with Garlic Parsley Pesto and
Wild Mushroom Cabernet Sauce**

Lemon Mascarpone Fresh Fruit Pizza

Wine Recommendations

1989 Orvieto Secco, Decugnano dei Barbi

1988 Merlot, Plum Creek Cellars, Colorado

1990 Moscato d'Oro, Robert Mondavi, Napa

"When Madeleine asked me to put together a menu for Friends for Dinner cookbook, I tried to think of a menu that I could match with wines. You can create a menu which will harmonize beautifully with wines by knowing a little bit about wine and foods and let your imagination run wild. This menu is from a winemaker dinner I have done for a special club." —Christopher DeJohn

Broiled Oysters Provencal

Serves 8

12 Roma tomatoes

4 Tbsp. olive oil

3 shallots, minced

1 1/2 Tbsp. garlic, minced

1/4 cup white wine

Salt and pepper to taste

Pinch of sugar

1/3 cup basil, chopped

32 Bluepoint oysters, shucked (your fishmonger
    will do this for you), reserve shells

1/3 cup sliced almonds

Basil sprigs, for garnish

Peel, seed and chop Roma tomatoes. In a medium-sized pan, over moderate heat, warm the olive oil. Sauté shallots and garlic, stirring until translucent. Add tomatoes and simmer for 10 minutes.

Add wine, salt and pepper and a pinch of sugar and simmer 5 more minutes. Add basil. Cool the mixture. (Sauce may be prepared the day before. Place in a bowl, cover and refrigerate.)

When ready to serve, preheat broiler. Place oysters back into their shells. Spoon about 1 tablespoon of tomato mixture over each oyster. Top with sliced almonds and broil for 2-3 minutes. (see Madeleine's Pantry)

May be served on a tray with rock salt and basil sprigs.

Imported Prosciutto Ham with Fresh Figs and Raspberries

Serves 8

2 baskets fresh raspberries

Juice of 1 lemon

Juice of 2 oranges

4 Tbsp. granulated sugar

1/3 cup water

16 thin slices of prosciutto ham

8 fresh figs, cut into quarters

Additional raspberries, for garnish

In a 1 quart saucepan over medium heat, place raspberries, lemon and orange juices, granulated sugar and water. Bring to a simmer, stirring occasionally, and simmer for 7 minutes. Purée. Transfer mixture to a bowl, cover and chill.

Presentation: Roll each slice of ham into a cone. Pour some of the chilled raspberry sauce over half of the plate. Place 2 ham slices in the center and one fig (cut in quarters) where there is no sauce. Place some fresh raspberries between figs. Repeat with remaining plates. These may be prepared ahead and kept refrigerated until serving time.

Colorado Tenderloin of Lamb with Garlic Parsley Pesto and Wild Mushroom Cabernet Sauce

Serves 8

3 1 lb. tenderloins of lamb, room temperature

Garlic Parsley Pesto

1/2 bunch parsley, rinsed, stems removed

2 cloves garlic, chopped

1/2 cup pine nuts

2 Tbsp. grated Parmesan cheese

3 ounces (6 Tbsp.) olive oil

14 turns pepper mill

Salt to taste

In a food processor, put parsley, garlic, pine nuts and Parmesan cheese. Start to purée. Slowly add olive oil until all is incorporated. Check for seasoning and add salt and pepper to taste. Transfer to a small container, cover and refrigerate for 1/2 hour.

Wild Mushroom Cabernet Sauce

2 Tbsp. shallots, minced

1 Tbsp. garlic, minced

8 ounces Shitake mushrooms, chopped

8 ounces tree oyster mushrooms, chopped

1 cup Cabernet Sauvignon wine

2 cups beef stock (see Madeleine's Pantry)

Salt and pepper to taste

In a heavy saucepan over medium-high heat, put remaining ingredients except stock and seasonings. Reduce by half the volume. Add stock and reduce again by half. Season with salt and pepper (this may be prepared ahead and kept warm in a thermos for 1 hour).

When ready to broil meat, preheat broiler. Lightly season lamb with salt and pepper. Make an incision down the middle of each tenderloin of lamb and spoon in some pesto. Broil, filling side up, for 12 to 15 minutes. (Do not overcook. Lamb should be served pink.)

Slice and serve warm with Wild Mushroom Cabernet Sauce.

Lemon Mascarpone Fresh Fruit Pizza

Serves 8

10 ounces mascarpone cheese

Juice of 1 lemon

Grated zest of 1 lemon

1/2 cup powdered sugar

1 16-ounce Boboli® pizza crust
  (available in supermarkets)

2 kiwi fruits, peeled and sliced

2 baskets fresh raspberries, picked over but not washed

2 baskets fresh blueberries, picked over but not washed

1 basket fresh strawberries, washed, trimmed and cut in half

1 cup apricot glaze (see Madeleine's Pantry)

In a small bowl with an electric mixer, put cheese, lemon juice, zest and powdered sugar. Mix well. Spread lemon cheese mix on pizza crust. Arrange slices of kiwi fruits in center of shell forming a circle. Continue making circles with strawberries (cut side down), then blueberries, ending with raspberries. Brush with apricot glaze.

Slice in wedges to serve.

Executive Chef Stephen Ford
Wellshire Inn

Built in 1926 as a clubhouse for the then-private Wellshire Country Club, this handsome English Tudor structure is, for many, one of Denver's significant landmarks. Wellshire Inn adjoins a 140 acre golf course and commands a superb view of the front range. At night, one can see the evening lights of downtown Denver on the distant horizon. The restaurant has seven dining rooms, each with a distinct character, ranging from intimate space for two to banquet rooms for several hundred.

Presiding over the kitchen is Executive Chef Stephen Ford. Early in life, Stephen realized that he wanted to be a part of the culinary world. To this end, he enrolled at the Culinary Institute at Hyde Park, New York. After eight months of study, he went to work for Winston Steiger at the Wilmington Country Club in Wilmington, Delaware. He credits this chef as having a great influence on his career. Four months later, he returned to the Institute with new vigor and a better understanding of the business. Upon graduation, he moved to Colorado to work at Pinehurst Country Club, then to California and finally back to Colorado. Each move marked a promotion in his career. In March of 1990, he was hired by Leo Goto, co-owner of the Wellshire Inn.

Fall Luncheon for Twelve People

Romaine, Radicchio and Watercress Salad with
Raspberry-Fig Vinaigrette

Grilled Striped Bass with Black Bean Sauce
Roasted Red Pepper Jalapeño Rouille

Baked Spaghetti Squash with Eggplant Caponata

Broccoli Florets

Pumpkin Cheesecake

Wine Recommendations

*1989 Dr. Burklin-Wolf Ruppertsberger
Reisling Kabinett, Rheinpfalz*

1989 Sancerre, Bonne Bouches, Bourgeois

"Enclosed is a menu and recipes for a luncheon that Leo and I did in Washington, D.C., recently, representing Project LEAN (Low-fat Eating for America Now). The luncheon was for the National Restaurant Association Marketing Executives Group. Leo Goto is the National Chairman of Food Professionals for Project LEAN. We both feel very strongly about lowering fat in the American diet. This menu has 880 calories, with only 25 percent of the calories from fat".
–Stephen Ford

Romaine, Radicchio and Watercress Salad with
Raspberry-Fig Vinaigrette

Raspberry-Fig Vinaigrette
Yield: 1 cup

6 canned figs

1 Tbsp. Dijon mustard

1/4 cup raspberry vinegar

1 tsp. fresh shallots, minced

1/2 tsp. black pepper

3 Tbsp. granulated sugar

1/4 cup extra virgin olive oil

Purée figs in food processor. Transfer fig purée to mixing bowl and add remaining ingredients except olive oil.

Slowly add oil, whipping constantly until all oil is incorporated.

Cover and refrigerate. Serve over approximately 12 cups of washed, dried and torn mixed greens: romaine, radicchio and watercress.

Grilled Striped Bass with Black Bean Sauce
Roasted Red Pepper Jalapeño Rouille

Serves 12

12 4-ounce fillets of striped bass
   (tuna or halibut may be substituted)

Brush fish lightly with 1 teaspoon olive oil. Season with salt and pepper.

Black Bean Sauce
Yield: 7 cups

1 lb. dried black beans*
2 dried ancho chilies, chopped
1 cup sundried tomatoes, chopped
1 slice bacon, chopped fine
2 cups onion, minced
1 tsp. granulated sugar
10 cups chicken stock
4 cloves garlic, minced
1/2 tsp. dried oregano
1 tsp. ground cumin
1 tsp. salt
2 slices lemon, seeds removed
2 Tbsp. sherry wine vinegar

Soak beans overnight in water to cover. Discard water.

Grill fish over charcoal, gas or woodburning grill until done. Approximately 3-4 minutes per side.

Serve with Black Bean Sauce and Roasted Red Pepper Jalapeño Rouille (recipes for both dishes follow).

Soak both ancho chilies and sundried tomatoes in hot water for approximately 10 minutes. Drain, chop.

Render bacon. Drain fat. Add onions, sugar, garlic and 1/4 cup of chicken stock and cook until vegetables are translucent. Add remaining ingredients except sherry wine vinegar and cook slowly, uncovered, stirring occasionally, until beans are very tender. It will take 3 to 4 hours. (This can be done a day ahead.)

Remove approximately half of the beans and process in a food processor until smooth. Add bean purée to the rest of the cooked beans and mix thoroughly. Add the sherry wine vinegar and mix well.

Suggested lean serving: scant 1/4 cup.

This sauce may be stored in the refrigerator for up to 5 days or frozen.

This sauce is used as a dip or served on any grilled fish or chicken.

Roasted Red Pepper Jalapeño Rouille
Makes 3/4 Cup

1/2 cup dry whole wheat breadcrumbs, soaked in 1/2 cup water

2/3 cup roasted red pepper (see Madeleine's Pantry)

1 Tsp. garlic, minced

1 Tsp. canned roasted jalapeño pepper

1 tsp. granulated sugar

2 Tsp. pure olive oil

Soak breadcrumbs in water

Purée roasted red pepper, garlic and jalapeño pepper in food processor until completely smooth.

Squeeze breadcrumbs. Add breadcrumbs and sugar to processor. Add olive oil in a thin stream while processor is runing.

Presentation: Place a pool of black bean sauce on each plate and put a 4-ounce grilled fish fillet on top; place 1 tsp. Red Pepper and Jalapeño Rouille on top of the fish.

Serves 12

2 large spaghetti squash

Heat oven to 350°F. Cut spaghetti squash in half and place cut side down on greased baking sheet. Do not cover. Bake for 45 minutes. Turn over, remove seeds carefully and continue baking for 10 minutes more or until squash is tender and can be easily pulled with a fork into strings.

Eggplant Caponata
Makes 8 cups

1 large yellow onion, diced

1 1/2 Tbsp. garlic, minced

1 Tbsp. shallots, minced

3 medium eggplants, diced (about 12 cups)

1/4 cup red wine

1/4 cup red wine vinegar

1/4 cup sugar

8 cups tomato sauce (2 quarts)

1/4 cup fresh oregano, chopped

1/2 cup fresh basil, chopped

In a non-stick pan sauté onions until soft in 2 teaspoons of water. Add garlic and shallots. Cook a few seconds. Add eggplant, red wine, red wine vinegar and sugar. Cook over medium heat for 15 minutes.

Add tomato sauce and herbs. Simmer for 20 to 25 minutes longer.

The caponata may be stored in the refrigerator for up to one week.

Presentation: Make a nest of spaghetti squash on each plate. Top with a serving of Eggplant Caponata.

It may also be used as a cold relish or served warm as a canape on garlic toast points topped with grated Asiago cheese.

Suggested lean serving: 1/4 cup

Broccoli Florets

Serves 12

2 large bunches of broccoli

Clean and cut broccoli into florets. Steam until desired tenderness.

Suggested lean serving: 1/2 cup florets as a side dish on plate.

Pumpkin Cheesecake

Makes 1 10-inch cake
Serves 16

1 1/2 cups graham cracker crumbs

2 Tbsp. sugar

1 egg white

1 lb. neufchatel cheese

1 1/2 cups sugar

4 Tbsp. cornstarch

4 egg whites

1 lb. fromage blanc

    (available in most supermarkets
    or in specialty foods stores)

1 1/2 cups mashed cooked or canned pumpkin

1/4 tsp. pumpkin pie spice

Preheat oven to 350°F.

Combine cracker crumbs, 2 Tbsp. sugar and 1 egg white and pack into the bottom of a 10 inch greased springform pan. Bake for 20 minutes or until the crumbs have set.

In the small bowl of an electric mixer, combine neufchatel cheese, sugar and cornstarch. Cream until smooth. Mixture will become lighter in color and will take on some volume.

With a fork or wire whisk, whip egg whites for a minute or so to lighten. Fold egg whites, fomage blanc and mashed pumpkin into mixture. Add pumpkin spice. Mix well. Pour over prebaked crust.

Bake at 350°F. for approximately 1 hour and 20 minutes or until set.

Allow to cool overnight. Remove sides from pan and slice.

Fruit Glaze

8 medium Granny Smith apples, cubed

1/4 cup sugar

3/4 cup sweet wine (Sauternes or other sweet wine)

2 tsp. arrowroot

1 tsp. cold water

In a non-stick sauté pan, toss cubed apples and sugar over medium heat for 10 minutes. Add wine and bring to a simmer. Dissolve arrowroot in cold water and add to mixture. Allow to cool.

Serve cheesecake with some of the fruit glaze on each plate.

Matt Franklin
240 Union Restaurant

Matt Franklin comes from a family which has always appreciated good food. His mother was an excellent cook and owner of many cookbooks. His parents traveled frequently on weekends and left Matt in charge of the kitchen and meal planning while they were gone. When he was in high school in San Diego, he began to read his mother's cookbooks and cook more seriously, not only for himself but for his friends.

Matt moved to Taos, New Mexico, when he was eighteen years old. His first job there was washing dishes at the Taos Country Club, followed by stints in several restaurants where he worked up from soups and sandwiches to more elaborate foods. Then he and his father opened and operated their own restaurant in the Taos area, the Fountain at El Patio.

After that experience, Matt worked with some excellent European chefs as head chef and manager in a number of Taos restaurants. Four years ago, he sent his resumé to Chef Jimmy Schmidt and his partner Michael McCarty of the former Rattlesnake Club in Denver. They were impressed and hired him. After Jimmy and Michael ended their partnership, Matt stayed on as executive chef for Michael.

Matt feels that his two years there gave him an incredible culinary experience. Jimmy Schmidt had trained in Europe and in this country with the well-known teacher Madeleine Kamman. Jimmy taught Matt creativity, the revolving menu concept and a cooking style which is predominately American with many Southwestern overtones. Michael owns Michael's in Santa Monica and New York and Adirondacks in Washington, D.C. From him, Matt learned California-style cuisine. As Matt says, "I never learned so much in two years."

During his days at the Rattlesnake Club, he worked with Noel Cunningham of Strings on several benefit dinner parties. Noel encouraged Matt to open his own restaurant someday. When the time came for such a venture, Noel and Michael Coughlin became partners with Chef Matt Franklin to create 240 Union Restaurant.

Matt has great respect for Noel Cunningham, who encourages him to experiment with his own style of cooking, which he defines as "New American" with eclectic overtones. Matt designs his food around taste, texture, temperature and color. He has a diversified menu and tries to make each dish a unique experience for the diner.

Le Déjeuner Sur L'Herbe (A Picnic in the Field)

Menu for Four

Arugula and Radicchio Salad

Crostini with Ricotta and Sausage Topping

Grilled Shrimp with Roasted Tri-Color Peppers
and Basil Viniagrette

Cheese and Fresh Fruit

Wine Recommendations

1989 Gewurztraminer, Hugel, Alsace

1990 Vin Gris de Cigare, Bonny Doon, Santa Cruz

"Whether enjoying an afternoon in the mountains or a day in Washington Park, the highlight of your picnic will be complement of food, wine and friends." —Matt Franklin

Arugula and Radicchio Salad

Serves 4

4 1/8-inch slices pancetta

3 small bunches arugula, cut julienne

1 medium head radicchio, shredded

3 hard-cooked eggs, coarsely chopped

1/4 cup extra virgin olive oil

1/4 cup red wine vinegar

Salt and pepper to taste

Cut pancetta into small strips. In a small sauté pan over moderate heat, sauté pancetta until it renders its fat.

In a salad bowl, place arugula, radicchio and eggs. Add pancetta and rendered fat, olive oil and vinegar. Toss. Correct seasoning with salt and pepper.

Serves 4

2 5-inch length sweet Italian sausages

4 Tbsp. water

1 cup fresh ricotta

2 Tbsp. grated Parmesan cheese

Salt and freshly ground black pepper to taste

16 lightly toasted bread rounds (crostini)

Remove sausages from casings and crumble.

In small sauté pan over medium heat, place crumbled sausage and water and cook, stirring occasionally until water evaporates. Continue cooking, stirring until sausage is lightly browned. Remove from heat, drain on paper towel and let cool.

Place ricotta in a bowl. Add the Parmesan cheese and beat with a wooden spoon until well mixed. Season with salt and pepper. Add crumbled sausage to the ricotta mixture and blend well. Spread some of the ricotta-sausage mixture on each crostini round and serve.

Grilled Shrimp with Roasted Tri-Color Peppers
and Basil Vinaigrette

Serves 4

Grilled Shrimp

1 lb. large shrimp, peeled and deveined
2 Tbsp. olive oil
Pinch salt and dash of pepper

Marinate shrimp in olive oil, salt and pepper. Refrigerate 1 hour.

Preheat broiler. Broil shrimp approximately 2 minutes per side, basting occasionally with the marinade. Remove and let cool.

1 each of red, yellow, green bell peppers, roasted, peeled, julienned (see Madeleine's Pantry)

Basil Vinaigrette

1/4 cup olive oil
Juice of 1 lemon
1 Tbsp. fresh garlic, chopped
1 cup fresh basil, chopped
Salt and pepper to taste

In a medium-size bowl, mix olive oil, lemon, garlic, basil, salt and pepper. Add peppers and shrimp. Toss well. Cover and refrigerate for 8 hours or overnight.

For dessert:

Choose an assortment of: Brie, Goat cheese, Havarti, Jarlsburg cheese and serve with fruit in season.

Heinz Fricker
La Chaumière.

German-born Heinz Fricker likes to recall his mother's prediction, "He will be a chef someday," and how much as a youngster he enjoyed helping with the cooking at home.

He started his culinary training after the second World War at the world famous Bayrischer Hof (Bavarian Court Hotel) in Munich, which had an exceptionally good staff, including one chef who had cooked for Kaiser Wilhelm.

But Heinz longed to learn the cooking and language of other countries, so he ventured to Switzerland, Spain and then back to Baden Baden in Germany. He enrolled in the "Chef's Exchange Program", which gave him the opportunity to study for a year at Shannon Airport. He also learned English and saw the Irish countryside.

His next stop was England, where he further broadened his education at different restaurants for six years. All the chefs in the better hotels and restaurants in England were either French or Italian, so he added these cuisines to his repertoire.

He still had a thirst for travel and learning and went to the Bahamas where he was hired at the British Colonial Hotel in Nassau. It is from there that he came to the United States.

After working for eight years in a restaurant on the East Coast, he and a friend decided to capitalize on their interest and knowledge of fine baked *goods. They bought a large bakery in Washington D.C. and, to their delight, the venture was a great success.*

But the time had come for Heinz to fulfill his ambition to own a restaurant. He traveled to Colorado, which reminded him of his beloved Bavaria. In 1975, he purchased La Chaumière, where he has been ever since.

This ninety-seat restaurant, located fifteen minutes from Lyons on the way to Estes Park, serves Continental Cuisine in a peaceful mountain setting. The patrons enjoy creations from Heinz' international repertoire while watching Eurasian deer roam outside.

Menu for Six

Salmon Tartar

Beef Tongue with Chanterelle Mushrooms

European Plum Tart

Wine Recommendations

1989 Schloss Vollrads Riesling Kabinett Halbtrocken

1985 Nuits-St-Georges, Les Boudots, Mongeard-Mugneret

Muscat de Beaumes de Venise

"These dishes are perfect for a fall dinner. The European plum tart is a great favorite of our patrons."
                                                                    –Heinz Fricker

Salmon Tartar

Serves 6

6 ounces very fresh King or Sterling salmon
1 egg yolk
4 Tbsp. olive oil
2 medium shallots, finely diced
1/2 cup fresh basil, chopped
Salt and freshly ground black pepper

Chop raw salmon in very small dice. Place in a glass bowl and add other ingredients. Mix well. Season with salt and pepper to taste. Serve immediately.

Excellent as an appetizer on slices of French bread or quarters of toast.

Serves 6

Beef Tongue

2 lbs. beef tongue

1 carrot, roughly chopped

1 small onion, roughly sliced

1 celery rib, roughly sliced

1 tsp. coarse salt

1 bouquet garni tied in cheesecloth (2 parsley sprigs, 1small
    imported bay leaf, 1/4 tsp. thyme, 1 tsp. salt, 1 clove
    garlic, unpeeled but roughly chopped)

Mushrooms

2 Tbsp. butter

1 shallot, finely diced

1 cup chanterelle mushrooms, sliced

1 cup beef stock (see Madeleine's Pantry)

1/2 cup heavy cream

2 Tbsp. cornstarch

1/4 cup Parmesan cheese, freshly grated

*Blanch beef tongue for 10 minutes in simmering water to cover; rinse and
wash in cold water.*

Place beef tongue in a Dutch oven and cover with water. Add carrot, onion, celery, salt and bouquet garni. Cover and simmer for 2 to 2 1/2 hours or until the tip of the tongue is tender. Peel tongue, trim it and cut into slices. Set aside.

Preheat oven to 375°F.

Melt butter in a small saucepan. Over moderate heat, sauté shallot and chanterelles, stirring for 5 minutes. Set aside.

In a small heavy saucepan, boil together beef stock, heavy cream and cornstarch, stirring occasionally, until mixture thickens.

Arrange tongue slices in a glass serving dish, cover with the chanterelle mushroom mixture, pour cream sauce over it and sprinkle with Parmesan cheese. Bake for 20 minutes.

Preheat broiler.

Just before serving, run the glass serving dish under the broiler for a few seconds to lightly brown the sauce. Serve at once with rice and a fresh garden salad.

Serves 6 to 8

Makes 1 9-inch tart

Pate Sucrée

1 1/3 cups all-purpose flour

2 Tbsp. sugar

1/4 tsp. salt

4 ounces (1 stick) cold unsalted butter, cut into bits

1 large egg yolk, beaten with 1 1/2 Tbsp. ice water

In a bowl, sift together the flour, sugar and salt. Add the butter and blend the mixture until it resembles coarse meal. Add yolk mixture, toss the mixture until the liquid is incorporated and form the dough in a ball. Reserve 1/3 cup of the dough. Dust remaining dough with flour and chill it, wrapped in plastic wrap, for 1/2 hour.

Plum Filling

2 lbs. Italian plums, halved and pitted

2 Tbsp. flour

4 Tbsp. sugar mixed with 3/4 tsp. cinnamon

Whipped cream (optional)

Preheat oven to 400°F.

Roll out the dough to 1/8-inch thickness on a lightly floured surface. Press it into a 9-inch tart pan with a removable fluted rim and press firmly against the sides of pan. Trim dough even with top of tart pan.

Arrange plums, cut side up in a circular fashion, from the outside to the inside, in the prepared tart pan.

Add the 2 Tbsp. flour to the 1/3 cup of reserved dough and crumble the mixture over the tart. Bake for 45 minutes.

Remove the tart from the oven and sprinkle the sugar-cinnamon mixture over the top. Allow to cool to room temperature before serving.

Serve with whipped cream if desired.

Chef Daniel Groen
The Palace Arms. The Brown Palace Hotel

The Brown Palace in Denver has been a distinctive downtown hotel since Henry C. Brown opened it in 1892. Today a national historic landmark, it is renowned for the majesty of its architecture as well as its famous guests: international leaders, celebrities and royalty. The hotel has impressive onyx-panelled walls and an atrium that soars past ornamented brass railings. Its beautiful Tiffany stained-glass ceiling dominates the entire setting and proclaims the hotel's Victorian heritage.

The Brown offers incomparable atmosphere to its patrons, from high tea in the lobby while listening to the melody of a harp or piano to a simple and relaxed meal in the Ship Tavern or an elegant dinner in the hauntingly beautiful Palace Arms. The latter, with its antique mirrors, muted lighting and numerous Napoleonic flags and memorabilia, is reminiscent of an era when dining was truly an art.

Presiding over the kitchen of the Palace Arms is Chef Daniel Groen. From Monterey, California, Daniel came to Denver to attend a mechanical school and financed his education by working in the kitchens of some of Denver's better restaurants. He washed dishes, made sandwiches and soon realized that the culinary field was his calling.

A friend who worked at The Broadmoor, in Colorado Springs, asked him if he would be interested in an apprenticeship in a private club. He accepted the invitation and enrolled at The Denver Club's day program, leading to the certificate of the "American Culinary Federation Approved Apprenticeship."

105

He graduated at the top of his class and was named "Apprentice of the Year." At the same time, Daniel apprenticed at night at the Denver Country Club. Tutored there by an American chef, he also acquired some knowledge of European-style cooking from their French and Swiss chefs.

Then he began to compete in national and international culinary shows. He was a member of the Western Regional Culinary Olympic Team which in 1988 won the national championship at a culinary show in Chicago. The same year, the team competed with 6,000 chefs for a period of ten days at the International Culinary Olympics in Frankfurt, Germany. Though only 29 years old and the youngest member of the team, Daniel won three silver medals and one bronze medal for hot and cold food and centerpiece competition.

Daniel joined The Brown Palace in 1989 as chef at the Ship Tavern and became chef at the Palace Arms in January, 1990. The food at the Palace Arms is very modern, upscale and eclectic. Daniel relies on his classical training, adds his own innovation and concentrates on making dishes lighter and appealing to the eye. Guests at the Palace Arms, a Mobil Four-Star establishment, will eat as they will not anywhere else.

"Being around talented people helps keep me going," says Daniel. His wife, Bonnie, is a "top ten graduate" of the Culinary Institute and a great inspiration to him.

Daniel Groen was nominated by his peers in 1989 for the award "Best Chef of the Year."

Menu for Six

Chilled Russian Ice House Soup "Stolichnaya"

Grilled Vegetable Salad with Sundried Tomato, Herb Balsamic
Vinaigrette

Seafood Ragout and Scallion Mornay Sauce

Pear Grape Tart with Vanilla Ice Cream

Wine Recommendations

1989 Gamay Noir, Amity, Oregon

1989 Pinot Noir, Saintsbury, Carneros

*"This menu is an example of the unusual fare of the Palace Arms. It is
excellent served on a warm summer evening."*   *–Daniel Groen*

Serves 6

1 1/2 Tbsp. olive oil

1 tsp. garlic, minced

1 rib celery, chopped

1/4 medium yellow onion, chopped

1 bay leaf

20 large shrimp, peeled, deveined, shells reserved

1 Tbsp. tomato paste

1/2 cup Chardonnay wine

1 cup water

1 cup sour cream

2 Tbsp. red onion, finely chopped

2 cups heavy cream

1/4 tsp. cayenne pepper

Pinch of sugar

1 tsp. salt or to taste

2 Tbsp. Stolichnaya Vodka

Juice of 1 lemon

4 Tbsp. fresh dill, minced

In a 2-quart saucepan over medium heat, warm 1 1/2 Tbsp. olive oil. Sauté garlic, celery and onion, stirring occasionally for 3 minutes. Add bay leaf, shrimp and shells and cook for 3 minutes more. Remove from heat and take shrimp out of the pan. Set aside.

Add tomato paste to saucepan, mix well. Return to heat and cook for 2 minutes. Add Chardonnay wine and water. Stir, raising heat to high, and continue cooking until reduced by 2/3. Strain stock, discard shells and reserve liquid. Cool slightly.

In food processor, purée 1/2 of the shrimp with 4 Tbsp. of stock. Add to reserved liquid along with sour cream, raw red onion, heavy cream and seasonings, Vodka, lemon juice and 3 Tbsp. of dill. Chill thoroughly.

Divide soup among 6 chilled bowls and garnish with remaining dill.

Grilled Vegetable Salad with Sundried Tomato
and Herb Balsamic Vinaigrette

Serves 6

Herb Balsamic Vinaigrette

2 Tbsp. balsamic vinegar

4 Tbsp. olive oil from sundried tomatoes (drain oil from jar)

4 Tbsp. good quality olive oil

1/2 Tbsp. garlic, minced

2 Tbsp. fresh basil, chopped

1 Tbsp. fresh mint, chopped

Juice of 1 lime

2 sprigs fresh oregano leaves, chopped

2 sprigs fresh thyme leaves, chopped

Salt and pepper to taste

Mix all above ingredients together in a jar. Correct seasoning and let stand for 4 hours at room temperature.

Grilled Vegetable Salad with Sundried Tomato

2 large red onions, sliced 1/2 inch thick

2 large yellow squash, sliced 1/2 inch thick

2 heads romaine lettuce, washed, leaves separated

2 sundried tomatoes in oil, drained and minced

Heat broiler. Oil broiler rack and grill onion and squash slices for 2 minutes on each side or until desired doneness is achieved. Grill romaine for 30 seconds. (Grilling may be done on charcoal grill in summer.)

Presentation: Lay grilled vegetables on plate, sprinkle sundried tomatoes over and drizzle with Herb Balsamic Vinaigrette.

Serves 6

Seafood Ragout

1 1/2 Tbsp. olive oil

12 large shrimp, peeled, deveined

12 large sea scallops

1 cup shitake mushrooms, stemmed, cleaned and chopped

Salt and pepper to taste

Juice of 1 lemon

12 mussels, cleaned and steamed open (see Madeleine's Pantry)

5 Tbsp. chives, minced

24 ounces cooked linguine, seasoned with salt and pepper and mixed with the chives

In a large skillet, heat olive oil over moderate heat. Add shrimp and scallops and cook, stirring for 3 minutes. Add mushrooms, stir well and cook 3 more minutes. Add dash of salt and pepper and lemon juice. Add cooked mussels and warm through. Remove from heat and keep warm.

Scallion Mornay Sauce

1 1/2 Tbsp. olive oil

2 tsp. garlic, minced

1/2 small yellow onion, finely chopped

1 quart heavy cream

1 cup fish stock (see Madeleine's Pantry)

1 tsp. Dijon mustard

1/4 tsp. nutmeg

1/4 cup white wine

3-ounces grated Parmesan cheese

2 small bunches scallions, cleaned and sliced thin

1/4 cup Sherry (or to taste)

In a large heavy saucepan, over medium-high heat, warm olive oil. Sauté garlic and onion, stirring for 2 minutes. Add cream, stock, seasonings and mix well. Continue cooking until reduced by 1/3. Add wine and cheese, stirring until cheese is fully incorporated. Add scallions and warm through.

Strain the solids, reserving the liquids. Purée the solids in a food processor or blender. Return the purée to the liquids and add Sherry. Stir. Remove from heat and set aside. Sauce may be prepared up to 1 hour ahead and reheated in a double boiler.

Presentation: Ladle 2-3 Tbsp. of warm sauce onto center of each plate and move sauce by tilting plate until bottom is covered. Place some pasta onto center of plate and arrange seafood around it. Pass the extra sauce.

Pear Grape Tart with Vanilla Ice Cream

Serves 6

1 recipe Pate Sucrée (see Madeleine's Pantry)
6 3-inch tartlet pans with removable fluted rim
3 Bartlett pears, peeled, cored, cut in half lengthwise
Juice of 1/2 lemon
1 1/2 cups red grapes, cut in half
Dash of cinnamon
Dash of nutmeg
1 1/2 Tbsp. granulated sugar
3/4 cup apricot glaze (see Madeleine's Pantry)
Vanilla ice cream

Preheat oven to 375°F.

Roll out dough 1/8" thick on a floured surface. Cut 6 4- to 5-inch circles and press each firmly into a tartlet pan. Chill the shells for 15 minutes. Slice each half pear across into 1/8" slices, keeping pear shape. Sprinkle with lemon juice.

Place slices of 1/2 pear in center of each tartlet. Arrange cut grapes around pear slices (cut side down).

Mix cinnamon, nutmeg and sugar and sprinkle over fruit.

Bake for 25 minutes. Remove from oven and brush with warm apricot glaze. Serve with your favorite vanilla ice cream.

Ross Johnson
Brick Oven Beanery

Ross Johnson, owner of the Brick Oven Beanery, worked as a waiter in a restaurant while studying for a degree in philosophy at the University of Minnesota. Since he knew it would be difficult to make a living as a philosopher, he opted to pursue a culinary career. But one other love claimed him first, mountain climbing. He became an expert, climbing in Switzerland and Scotland, and became one of the first Americans to accomplish a Scottish Grade Five in ice climbing.

Returning to America in 1971, Ross enrolled in a hotel-training program offered by the Radisson Hotel chain headquartered in Minneapolis. During this course of study, he developed a concept of casual dining for Radisson restaurants which became known as the "Haberdashery Style."

When his boss at the Radisson was named Vice President of Food and Beverage for the Ramada Inn Hotels in Phoenix, Arizona, Ross went along as his assistant. It was quite a move for Ross. As he says, "I went from being a climbing bum to the assistant vice president for a chain of 700 hotels."

After three years, he came to Denver where he went to work for the Mr. Steak enterprise and then on to a three-year stint as Vice President of the Hoffman House Restaurants, headquartered in Chicago.

Mountains still beckoned, so in 1983, Ross moved to a home in Sun Valley and opened his own restaurant, the Brick Oven Beanery, in Boise, Idaho. A year and a half later, he opened a twin of that eatery in Denver. Both have been successful. Ross says, "We work hard at catering to the mixed lunch crowd that we have and to families who frequent the restaurant at night, attracted by the reasonably priced children's menu."

The kitchen runs as systematically as possible. There is no chef per se; three people share responsibility of the operation. His carefully developed recipes are to be followed exactly. He even had a graphic artist design a "dice chart" for all vegetables so the staff would know exactly how the final product should look.

The food at the Beanery is delicious. Everything is made from scratch, and bread is baked daily on the premises. Despite its "cafeteria line," every attempt is made to avoid a fast-food atmosphere. The comfortable chairs, programmed music and subdued lighting all contribute to a relaxed atmosphere. "We don't try to be elegant and pretentious," Ross adds, "but rather, comfortable."

Saturday Night Dinner Menu for eight

Mixed Green Salad with Pepper Parmesan Dressing

Wild Rice Meat Loaf

Buttermilk Mashed Potatoes

Roasted Onion Mushroom Gravy

Roasted Corn on the Cob

Fresh Strawberry Shortcake on Chocolate Biscuits

Wine Recommendations

1982 Dom Perignon in Plastic Cups

1987 Merlot, Reserve, Columbia Crest, Washington

"At the Brick Oven Beanery we whimsically refer to our food as being 'like Mom tried to cook.' In fact, we do take old, familiar family dishes, much like many of us grew up with, and add a bit of update flair. In this particular menu you will find a substantial Saturday Night Dinner of comfort dishes with some unique twists." —Ross Johnson

Mixed Green Salad with Pepper Parmesan Dressing

Serves 8

Salad

1 head romaine lettuce

1 head bib lettuce

2 heads curly endive

Tear greens into pieces and wash in cold water. Dry completely and chill. Place in large bowl. Just prior to serving, toss gently with Pepper Parmesan Dressing and let sit for 1 minute.

Pepper Parmesan Dressing
Makes about 1 3/4 cups

1 cup mayonnaise, preferably homemade

1 Tbsp. fresh lemon juice

1/4 cup parsley, finely minced

1 Tbsp. A-1 Sauce

1 Tbsp. Worcestershire Sauce

1 clove garlic, minced

1 Tbsp. Dijon mustard

1 tsp. freshly ground black pepper

1 tsp. honey

1/4 cup grated Parmesan cheese

1/2 tsp. anchovy, minced (optional)

In a bowl, mix ingredients in order given with a wire whip. Refrigerate until ready to use.

Serves 8

2 lbs. ground beef

1 cup cooked wild rice

3/4 cup fine breadcrumbs

2 eggs

1 tsp. salt

1 clove garlic, minced

1 tsp. black pepper

1/4 tsp. nutmeg

1/4 cup fresh parsley, chopped

1 tsp. Worcestershire Sauce

1 tsp. catsup

1 tsp. prepared horseradish

Preheat oven to 350°F.

Mix ingredients in order given. Shape into a loaf. Lay a piece of aluminum foil on work counter and place meatloaf on it. Roll meatloaf lightly in foil and refrigerate for 1/2 hour. Remove foil and bake for 1 hour on a lightly greased baking sheet.

Serves 8

3 lbs. potatoes, scrubbed and quartered, skin on

1/4 cup (1/2 stick) butter, room temperature

1 tsp. salt

1 tsp. black pepper

1/2 cup buttermilk

Milk for desired consistency

Cook potatoes in boiling water until barely tender. Mash potatoes while still hot with remaining ingredients, leaving slightly lumpy.

2 yellow onions, sliced

2 carrots, julienned

1/2 cup water

1 cup dry red wine

1/2 cup flour

1/2 cup (1 stick) butter, melted

2 cups beef stock (see Madeleine's Pantry)

1/2 tsp. dried thyme

1/2 tsp. dried rosemary

1 cup mushrooms, chopped

Salt and pepper to taste

Preheat oven to 350°F. Put onions, carrots and water in a non-stick pan and roast for 1 1/2 hours or until deeply caramelized. Remove vegetables from pan and set aside. Over high heat, deglaze pan with red wine, scraping up any browned bits in pan. Set aside. In a small ovenproof pan, mix flour and melted butter together, making a roux. Bake roux for 15 minutes.

In a large pan over medium heat, warm stock, herbs and mushrooms. Purée onions and carrots in a food processor and add to roux mixture. Stir vegetables and roux mixture into stock, herbs and mushrooms. Add red wine from roasting pan and enough hot water to desired consistency. Season with salt and pepper.

Serves 8

8 ears of fresh corn

Preheat oven to 350°F. Remove as much silk as possible while leaving husks intact. Place ears of corn on a cookie sheet and roast for 45 minutes. Pull husks back and trim to 2 inches (they will serve as a nice handle).

Serves 8

1 quart strawberries

1/2 cup sugar

2 ounces Grand Marnier

Wash and hull strawberries. Cut larger berries into halves, add sugar and Grand Marnier. Toss gently and let stand refrigerated, for 1 hour.

Chocolate Biscuits
Makes 8 biscuits

1 3/4 cups unbleached all-purpose flour

1 Tbsp. baking powder

2 Tbsp. sugar

3 Tbsp. cocoa powder

1/2 tsp. salt

5 Tbsp. unsalted butter, chilled, cut up

3/4 cup half-and-half

1 cup heavy cream, whipped and sweetened

Preheat oven to 450°F. Combine dry ingredients in a bowl. Cut butter into the dry ingredients, using a pastry blender or two knives. When ingredients are the consistency of cornmeal, add the half-and-half, gently mixing and form a ball.

Turn dough onto a floured board. Knead gently for a few seconds. Pat to a 3/4 inch thick sheet.

Using a 3-inch glass, cut 8 circles. Place close together on a lightly greased cookie sheet and bake for 12 to 15 minutes.

Presentation: Halve biscuits. Layer as follows: Biscuit, strawberries, whipped cream, biscuit, strawberries, whipped cream.

Joanne Katz
Three Tomatoes Catering

Three Tomatoes, one of Denver's premier catering firms, has been satisfying the tastes of happy patrons for the past fifteen years. Heading this successful business are Joanne Katz and her partner, Peggy Neusteter. Joanne, the contributing chef to this book, has always loved to cook, yet she never dreamed she would make a profession of it. Both her grandmothers were excellent cooks. Both were from Eastern Europe and prepared a cuisine different from anything her friends had experienced. She fondly remembers the fruit dumplings her Bohemian grandmother served for lunch in the summer.

In the ethnic neighborhood of Chicago where she grew up, cuisine was an important way of communicating the traditions of the "old country." One learned to like and appreciate the food of your native country and which market carried the proper ingredients.

College life brought Joanne to Colorado State University in Fort Collins, where she majored in English literature and philosophy. In Denver, she met Peggy Neusteter, who had gone to Colorado University as a psychology major. Though both women worked after graduation, it was not until later, as young mothers in need of a change in careers, that they decided to reassess their talents. On Joanne's suggestion, they started a catering company.

125

They booked a party. It was a success. They booked three more. After that, there never was much doubt whether they would continue. To quote Joanne, "Three Tomatoes Catering has been a success far beyond our dreams, but far more important than the business aspect of it, is the fact that it has been a rewarding personal relationship for two friends. Of that, I am most proud." She adds, "We work hard for and with our clients. One of our criteria is to personalize each party, to make it a unique occasion for the individual client."

A Sunday Brunch Menu for Six

Sliced Melons

Dove Breast with Polenta and Kalamata Olive Sauce

Tomato Salad

Wine Recommendations

1990 Dry Riesling, Chateau Ste. Michelle, Washington

1988 Nebbiolo d'Alba, Renato Ratti

"This menu was inspired by my husband, who is both an organic vegetable gardener and an avid hunter. The challenge to cook foods with the lavish raw materials he provides me is always rewarding. The idea of dove for breakfast came from a pastry chef, Alece, at Three Tomatoes. She is from Alabama and her family frequently has game birds for breakfast." —Joanne Katz

Sliced Melons

Use an assortment of Crenshaw, Cantaloupe and Honeydew.

Peel melons, seed and slice.
Place on a platter and garnish with fresh edible flowers.

Tomato Salad

Serves 6

6 small tomatoes, peeled, seeded and sliced

1 Tbsp. olive oil

1 tsp. balsamic vinegar

Salt and freshly ground pepper

Chopped fresh parsley, for garnish

Place tomato slices on a platter and drizzle with olive oil and vinegar.
Add salt and pepper to taste. Sprinkle parsley over tomatoes.

Serves 6

Dove Breast

3 Tbsp. olive oil

3 Tbsp. shallots, minced

6 dove breasts, removed from bone

   (May be prepared with either pheasant or duck breasts.)

1/4 cup freshly grated Romano cheese

In heavy sauté pan, heat olive oil over moderate-high heat. Add shallots and cook, stirring until soft. Add dove breasts and sauté for approximately 7 to 10 minutes. Do not overcook. Dove breasts should be slightly pink. Remove from pan; slice on the bias.

Polenta

3 cups milk

1 Tbsp. unsalted butter

1 tsp. sugar

1/2 tsp. salt

1 cup yellow cornmeal, preferably stone ground

   (available in health food stores.)

3 Tbsp. grated Parmesan cheese

2 Tbsp. unsalted butter, room temperature

   (available in health food stores.)

In a heavy pan, over moderate-heat, bring milk, 1 Tbsp. butter, sugar and salt to simmer. Slowly add cornmeal in a thin stream, whisking constantly. Lower heat and stir with wooden spoon until mixture is thickened and leaves the sides of the pan, about 10 minutes.

Add cheese and 2 Tbsp. butter. Place in a 9" cake pan and cool slightly. Unmold and cut in wedges to serve.

Kalamata Olive Sauce
Makes about 1 1/2 cups

2 Tbsp. olive oil

1 1/2 cups Kalamata olives, pitted and chopped

5 sundried tomatoes in olive oil, drained and chopped

1/2 yellow onion, finely chopped

2 cloves garlic, minced

1/4 tsp. red pepper flakes

1 tsp. fresh rosemary, chopped

1 Tbsp. fresh marjoram, chopped

2 Tbsp. fresh parsley, chopped

5 Tbsp. olive oil

1/2 cup dry red wine

2 Tbsp. capers

In a medium-size sauté pan over moderate heat, warm 2 Tbsp. olive oil. Sauté olives, tomatoes, onion, garlic and red pepper flakes until soft. Add rosemary, marjoram, parsley, 5 Tbsp. olive oil, wine and capers. Cook until reduced by 1/3.

Note: This sauce can be made ahead, doubled and used for pastas, soups, meat and sandwiches. If sauce is used for pasta, add 2 Tbsp. olive oil, 2 Tbsp. more parsley and some Parmesan cheese.

Ira Meyer
The Normandy

Ira Meyer grew up in a richly ethnic, extended family in the South Bronx of New York City. His grandparents were Russian immigrants who lived with his family. They did not believe in buying processed food but rather in "preparing everything yourself." His grandfather made beer, wine and root-beer in the basement. His grandmother made her own bread, pickles and liqueur. Ira vividly remembers that every Friday she faithfully rose early, covered the furniture with white sheets and proceeded to make fresh noodles, drying them on the sheets.

One of his fondest memories is eating raw fish left over from a dish his grandmother prepared for Passover. Thus he learned to eat and love "sushi" before it became today's popular Asian import.

Ira knew that his calling was in the food industry. He enrolled at the Culinary Institute in Hyde Park, New York, and graduated in 1978. Since then, he has worked in a variety of establishments, such as Café des Artistes and the Russian Tea Room, in New York City. He was involved in corporate dining at Merrill Lynch World Headquarters and Exxon World Headquarters in New York, as well as meal preparation at Colgate and Fordham universities.

Macy's Department Store in New York City afforded Ira a great learning experience. For four years in their food department, he operated restaurants, created recipes, helped open up accounts and purchased products for what they call "The Cellar," a section of the store devoted completely to food. This was the first time any department store in the United States had established an area such as this.

From New York, he came to Denver, where he has been chef at Normandy Restaurant since March of 1990. One of the first things that he did in concert with owner Karen Wolfe was to lighten the menu by using less fat and butter. In line with this thinking, the bistro Chez Michèlle, a newly-opened section of the restaurant, features more grilled items, pasta and other light fare. Both Karen and Ira hope that the customers will realize that this is healthy as well as tasty for them.

Menu for Six

Shrimp with Two Melon Salad, Green Peppercorn Lemon Vinaigrette

Sautéed Lobster with Tarragon Champagne Beurre Blanc

Herbed Fettucini

Asparagus Steamed with Lillet

Strawberries with a Bowl of Confectioner's Sugar and a Bowl of Balsamic Vinegar

Wine Recommendations

Roederer Estate California Sparkling Wine, Anderson Valley

1989 Domaine de Chevalier Blanc, Pessac-Leognan

1989 Maximiner Grunhaus Herrenberg Riesling Auslese, Mosel-Saar-Ruwer

"The following menu was planned to honor my friend, John Moroney. Unfortunately since the start of this project, he has fallen victim to this devastating disease, AIDS. What was to be a celebration of the present has become a remembrance of good times. John, wherever you are, keep smiling and spreading your love." —*Chef Ira Meyer*

Shrimp with Two Melon Salad, Green Peppercorn Lemon Vinaigrette

Serves 6

Salad

1 tsp. salt

1 lb. large shrimp, peeled and deveined

1/2 honeydew melon

1/2 cantaloupe melon

In a heavy pan, over medium-high heat, bring 1 gallon of water to a boil. Add 1 tsp. salt. Add shrimp, stirring until water returns to a boil. Immediately, take off heat and allow to sit for 5 minutes. Drain and rinse with ice water. Drain well. Place shrimp in a bowl, cover and refrigerate until ready to use.

Peel and seed melons and cut each into 18 thin slices (allow 3 slices of honeydew and cantaloupe per person).

Green Peppercorn Lemon Vinaigrette

Juice of 1 lemon

3 ounces (6 Tbsp.) canola oil

Grated zest of 1/2 lemon

1 Tbsp. white wine vinegar

1 Tbsp. green peppercorns, packed in brine,
    drained, rinsed and crushed

Salt and pepper to taste

1 Tbsp. parsley, chopped (for garnish)

Combine all ingredients for vinaigrette in a jar and adjust seasoning, if needed. Pour vinaigrette over the shrimp to coat lightly. Mix well.

Presentation: Alternate slices of melon on individual cold plates. Arrange shrimp over the melon, down the center of the plate. Drizzle any remaining dressing over the melon and shrimp. Garnish with parsley. This is especially beautiful served on black plates.

Sautéed Lobster with Tarragon Champagne
Beurre Blanc & Herbed Fettucini

Serves 6

1 cup Champagne

4 ounces (1 stick) unsalted butter

4 8-ounce lobster tails, shell removed,
    lobster sliced into medallions

4 whole shallots, finely minced

1/2 red bell pepper, seeded and diced

1 1/4 cups heavy cream

1 Tbsp. fresh tarragon, chopped

1/2 tsp. pink peppercorns, crushed

Salt and pepper to taste

1/2 lb. fettucine

1 Tbsp. chives, minced

4 Tbsp. parsley, chopped

In a small nonreactive saucepan, over medium-high heat, reduce the Champagne to 1/4 cup. Set aside.

Heat butter in a large skillet, over high heat. When foam subsides, add lobster and sauté, stirring for 3 minutes (do not overcook). Remove lobster from pan and set aside. Add shallots and sauté for 1 minute. Add diced red bell pepper, heavy cream and reduced Champagne. Stir and bring to a boil. Reduce by 1/3. Add tarragon, pink peppercorns and lobster. Mix well. Season with salt and pepper.

In a heavy pan over high heat, bring 2 quarts of water to a boil. Add 1 tsp. salt and cook fettucine pasta until al dente. Drain well and mix with chives and 1 tablespoon parsley.

Presentation: Place the fettucine on a large serving platter. Make a well in the center and pour sautéed lobster with tarragon Champagne butter sauce in the center of the fettucine. Sprinkle the entire platter with remaining chopped parsley. Serve immediately.

Asparagus Steamed with Lillet

Serves 6

2 lbs. asparagus, cleaned
1 cup water
1 cup white Lillet
   (available in liquor stores)

Place water and Lillet in the bottom of steamer basket. Bring to boil and add asparagus. Cover and steam for about 8 to 10 minutes, or until cooked as desired.

Strawberries with a Bowl of Confectioner's Sugar and a Bowl of Balsamic Vinegar

Serves 6

3 pints strawberries, cleaned and stemmed
1 cup confectioner's sugar
1/2 cup balsamic vinegar

Pass bowl of strawberries. Sprinkle each serving with some balsamic vinegar and generously dust with confectioner's sugar.

Luc Meyer
The Left Bank

By the time Luc Meyer was 14 years old, his parents had exposed him to the truly "good food" in most of the three-star restaurants of France. His mother is a great cook; his grandfather was the top patissier in Strasbourg, and their love of the craft affected his decision to make cooking his life's work.

By the time Luc was 17, he had begun the long, hard road toward becoming a chef. The trouble was that his parents did not take his decision seriously. His first apprenticeship was at the Pyramide in Vienne, considered by many the temple of French gastronomy. He spent the summer there, and when his parents came to get him, he would not leave. That was when they believed him.

From the Pyramide, it was on to the renown three-star l'Oustau de Baumanière in Les Baux-en-Provence, where he stayed for three years working under owner-chef Raymond Thuillier. By 1966, Luc had worked in France, Switzerland, Canada and the Virgin Islands.

On a vacation to the Rocky Mountains in July, 1970, Luc and his wife, Liz, fell in love with the area. Two months later, they returned to Vail to settle. Today, Luc is the chef-owner of the Left Bank Restaurant.

The cuisine at the Left Bank has changed since its opening, continually influenced by Luc's travels. The restaurant has become as famous as some of its guests who include former President Gerald Ford, Pierre Elliott Trudeau, Walter Mondale, John Denver, Robert Redford and Joan Rivers.

Menu for Six

Vichyssoise (Chilled Leek-Potato Soup)

Salade de Tomates (Sliced Tomato Salad)

Filet de Sole Véronique (Fillet of Sole with
Grapes and Cream Sauce)

Epinards en Branche (Fresh Leaf Spinach)

Tarte et Sorbet Aux Myrtilles du Michigan
(Michigan Blueberry Tart and Sorbet)

Wine Recommendations

1985 Riesling, Cuvée Frederic Emile, Trimbach

1985 Corton-Bressandes, Tollot-Beaut

1989 Erdener Pralat, Dr. Loosen, Mosel-Saar-Ruwer

The following menu was taken from The Left Bank Celebrity Cookbook by Luc Meyer. It was served during the first annual Gerald Ford Golf Tournament in June, 1977.

"The 'plats' are part of a dinner menu created one evening for former President Ford and Mrs. Ford's party. The Tarte aux Myrtilles du Michigan (Michigan blueberry tart) is a favorite of Mr. Ford."

—Luc Meyer

Vichyssoise (Chilled Leek-Potato Soup)

Serves 6

2 medium-sized red potatoes

Salt to taste

2 cups chicken stock (see Madeleine's Pantry)

2 tender young leeks

1 egg yolk

1 cup heavy cream

Pepper

2 Tbsp. chopped fresh chives

Peel the potatoes and cut in 1 inch cubes. Place in a 2 quart saucepan with salt and 1 cup stock. Bring to a boil, reduce heat and simmer for 15 minutes or until the potatoes are partially cooked.

While potatoes are cooking, discard the dark green leaves of the leeks and cut the leeks in half, lengthwise. Wash thoroughly, drain and cut into thin slices. Add the leeks and the remaining stock to the potatoes and increase the heat to high. Cook for another 5 to 10 minutes or until the leeks and potatoes are completely cooked. Remove pan from heat and let the soup cool slightly.

Strain the solids, reserving the liquid, and purée in the processor. Return purée to the liquid in the pan, over low heat. Beat the egg yolk with the heavy cream until thoroughly mixed and gradually whisk this mixture into the hot soup. Continue cooking the soup over low heat, stirring continuously, until it thickens slightly (do not allow to boil).

Pour the soup through a fine-meshed sieve, season with salt and pepper and chill in the refrigerator. Just prior to serving, stir in the chives.

Serve in chilled cups. (Vichyssoise will keep 2 to 3 days in the refrigerator but tastes best when served the same day it is made.)

Serves 6

Salad

small, fresh, ripe tomatoes, sliced
1 medium-sized red onion, finely chopped
1/2 bunch parsley, stems discarded, finely chopped
1/3 cup Sauce Vinaigrette (recipe follows)

Arrange the tomato slices on chilled salad plates. Sprinkle the tomato slices with the onion and some parsley. Spoon Sauce Vinaigrette on top and garnish with remaining parsley.

Sauce Vinaigrette
Makes 1 1/2 cups

1/3 cup red wine vinegar
1/2 tsp. salt
Freshly ground black pepper
1 cup olive oil
1 tsp. finely chopped parsley, tarragon or other fresh herbs
1 Tbsp. Dijon mustard (optional)
1 Tbsp. shallots, minced

Combine all the ingredients in a jar with a screw top and shake vigorously for 30 seconds or until the sauce emulsifies. This vinaigrette may be kept in the refrigerator for several days.

Filet de Sole Véronique
(Fillet of Sole with Grapes and Cream Sauce)

Serves 8

8 4-ounce sole fillets

3/4 cup plus 2 Tbsp. butter

1 small shallot, finely chopped

3 cups fish stock (see Madeleine's Pantry)

1 cup heavy cream

Salt and freshly ground white pepper to taste

Few drops fresh lemon juice

28 Thompson seedless grapes, peeled

Flatten the sole fillets to a thickness of 1/2 inch with a cleaver and roll each fillet up to form a cylinder.

Butter a heavy sauté pan with 2 Tbsp. butter and add the shallot and rolled-up fish fillets. Add fish stock, cover the pan and cook on the stove at a gentle simmer until the fish flakes when pressed, about 10 minutes. Carefully transfer the fish cylinders to a serving dish, cover with a piece of buttered foil and keep warm.

Boil the poaching liquid from the fish until only 1/2 cup liquid remains. Add the cream and continue boiling to reduce the sauce by half.

Remove the pan from the heat and whisk in the remaining butter, a little bit at a time, to obtain a smooth, silky sauce. Season with salt and pepper and a few drops of lemon juice. (The sauce may be kept warm over a pot of hot water.)

Serves 6

3 lbs. fresh leaf spinach

4 Tbsp. (1/2 stick) butter

Salt and pepper to taste

Wash spinach in cold water, changing the water 2 or 3 times, or until the spinach is clean.

Bring salted water to a boil in a large, non-aluminum pot and add the spinach. Cook 2 minutes. Transfer the spinach to a colander and refresh the leaves under cold running water until the spinach is completely cool.

Squeeze the spinach leaves in a dish towel to wring out as much water as possible. Place on a plate, cover and refrigerate. (It will keep this way for 2 to 3 days in the refrigerator.)

Prior to serving, heat the butter in a heavy sauté pan. Add the spinach and cook until hot, stirring occasionally. Season with salt and pepper.

Tarte et Sorbet Aux Myrtilles du Michigan
(Michigan Blueberry Tart and Sorbet)

Serves 6 to 8

Makes 1 9-inch tart

Pate Sucrée (see Madeleine's Pantry)
4 cups fresh blueberries, picked over but not washed
Confectioner's sugar
Blueberry Sorbet (recipe follows)

Roll the Pate Sucrée to a thickness of 3/16-inch and line a 9-inch tart pan with removable bottom. Cut off the excess dough. Prick the bottom of the crust with a fork.

Preheat oven to 450°F.

Fill the tart shell with blueberries until the berries are flush with the top of the crust. Bake in preheated oven for 35 minutes or until the crust is cooked. Remove tart from the oven and let cool on wire rack.

Unmold the tart and sprinkle with confectioner's sugar for serving.

This tart should be served the day it is cooked and not refrigerated.

Blueberry Sorbet

2 cups fresh blueberries, picked over but not washed
1 1/4 cups sugar
Juice of 1/2 lemon
5 ounces cold water

Purée the blueberries with sugar, lemon juice and water in a blender or processor. Pour this mixture into an ice cream machine and churn, according to the manufacturer's directions, until smooth and frozen. Serve this sorbet the day it is made.

Presentation: Place wedges of tarte on dessert plates with a scoop of Blueberry Sorbet to the side.

Matthew Meyers
La Coupole

"La Coupole, Bonjour!" This is the cheery greeting one receives when making a reservation at this delightful French restaurant in lower-downtown Denver. Located in the historic Paris Hotel building (until recently an abandoned monument to the decay in big cities) La Coupole is the creation of French brothers Philippe and Pierre Muraz. Their tasteful and elegant renovation earned them a 1991 award from the Denver Partnership, an organization promoting the preservation and improvement of downtown Denver.

Matthew Meyers heads the kitchen here, pursuing his life-long ambition as a chef, as he states, "A desire to work with my hands and be creative in the sense of making other people happy." Early in his career, Matthew felt that European classical training would help him reach his goal. Therefore, he enrolled at the well-known international school, Ecole de Cuisine Française, in Sussex, England. The director of the school, Sabine de Mirbeck, is the daughter-in-law of Madame Brassard, who ran the Cordon Bleu Cooking School in Paris for years.

After graduation, he worked in England at a two-star Michelin restaurant before being hired as sous-chef at La Coupole. He took over the complete operation there in 1991. True to the atmosphere at La Coupole, he characterizes the restaurant's cuisine as "country cooking with elegance." Judging by the success of the French eatery, Matthew and his staff are going in the right direction.

Menu for Six

Crème Renversée de Mais et Coquilles St. Jacques avec Sauce
Curry et Poblano Peppers (Flan of Scallops and Corn with
Curry Sauce and Poblano Peppers)

Veau à la Jurassienne avec Sauce Diable (Medallions of
Veal en Croûte, Sauce Diable)

Gratinée aux Poires, Sabayon au Stilton
(Gratin of Pears, Stilton Sabayon)

Wine Recommendations

1990 Muscadet Marquis de Goulaine

1985 Chateauneuf-du-Pape, Chateau de Beaucastel

1983 Chateau Filhot, Sauternes

"These are some of my favorite dishes"   —Matthew Meyers

Crème Renversée de Maïs et Coquilles
St. Jacques avec Sauce Curry et Poblano Peppers (Flan of
Scallops and Corn with Curry Sauce and Poblano Peppers)

Serves 6

Flan of Scallops

1 1/2 Tbsp. butter

1/2 cup yellow onion, chopped

1 cup frozen whole kernel corn, defrosted

1/2 cup dry Vermouth

8-ounces sea scallops, sliced

3 eggs

1 1/2 cups heavy cream

1/2 cup fresh poblano peppers, minced

Curry Sauce and Poblano Peppers (recipe follows)

Whole chives, for garnish

In a sauté pan over moderate heat, melt butter. Sauté onion until translucent. Add corn and cook, stirring for 1 minute. Add dry Vermouth and reduce to nearly dry. Set aside to cool.

Preheat oven to 350°F.

Oil 6 ramekins (3/4 cup each) and line the bottom and the sides of them with the sea scallops.

Purée corn mixture in a processor and pour it into a bowl. Add the eggs, cream and poblano peppers. Divide mixture among the ramekins. Cover each with a piece of foil. Place them in a flat baking dish with hot water half way up sides of ramekins and bake for 30 to 35 minutes. Let cool. Refrigerate for 8 hours or overnight.

Curry Sauce and Poblano Peppers

1 1/2 Tbsp. butter
1/2 cup fresh poblano peppers, minced
Pinch ground curry
3/4 cup heavy cream
1/3 cup plain yogurt

In a sauté pan, melt 1 1/2 Tbsp. butter and sauté poblano peppers until soft. Add pinch of curry and cook, stirring for 1 minute. Add cream and continue cooking until thick. Cool. Add yogurt and stir well.

Presentation: Invert each flan onto a serving plate and spoon sauce around it. Garnish with whole chives.

Veau à la Jurassienne avec Sauce Diable
(Medallions of Veal en Croûte, Sauce Diable)

Serves 6

Medallions of Veal

12 squares of puff pastry (roughly the shape
    of veal medallions, plus 1/2 inch border)
Egg wash (1 egg yolk beaten with 1 tsp. cold water)
Duxelles (recipe follows)
6 4-ounce medallions of veal, 1/2-inch thick
    (from top round of veal)
Salt and pepper to taste
2 Tbsp. butter
3 thin slices prosciutto ham, halved
6 slices Gruyère cheese, julienned
Sauce Diable (recipe follows)
Parsley sprigs, for garnish

Lay out puff pastry squares on greased cookie sheet. Brush tops with egg wash and chill for 1/2 hour.

Season the veal medallions with salt and pepper. In large skillet, melt 2 Tbsp. butter over high heat. Add veal and sauté until golden, about 2 minutes, turning medallions once. Lower heat to low, cover pan and cook for 2 minutes. Transfer veal to a platter. Cover and chill.

Duxelles

1 Tbsp. butter
2 1/2 Tbsp. shallots, minced

2 cups mushrooms, finely chopped

1/2 cup red bell pepper, diced

Salt and pepper to taste

Heat butter in large skillet over medium-high heat. Add shallots, mushrooms and red bell pepper. Sprinkle with salt and pepper and cook, stirring for 8 minutes. Put mixture in a small bowl. Cover and chill.

Sauce Diable

1 Tbsp. butter

1 clove garlic, minced

2 1/2 Tbsp. shallots, minced

1/2 cup red bell pepper, diced

2 Tbsp. red wine vinegar

1/3 cup red wine

1 1/2 cups veal stock (see Madeleine's Pantry)

2 Tbsp. butter, softened

In sauté pan over moderate heat, melt 1 Tbsp. butter. Sauté garlic, shallots and red bell pepper until soft. Add vinegar and cook until nearly dry. Raise heat, add red wine and reduce by 1/2. Add stock and reduce by 1/3. Strain the solids, reserving the liquid. Purée the solids in a blender. Return the purée to the liquid. Add the softened butter and stir. Season with salt and pepper.

To assemble the puff pastry squares: Divide duxelles by 6 and spread on 6 chilled pastry squares, leaving 1/2 inch border on all sides. Lay a pre-cooked veal medallion in center of each square. Top with 1/2 ham slice and julienne of Gruyère. Brush edges (not sides) of pastry squares with egg wash mixture. Top each medallion with another pastry square. Press edges of pastry firmly to seal. Brush pastry tops with egg wash and place pan in refrigerator for 1/2 hour.

Preheat oven to 425°F. Bake medallions of veal on center rack of oven until golden brown, about 15 minutes.

Presentation: Reheat sauce. Serve each Medallion en Croûte surrounded with sauce and garnished with parsley. Serve remaining sauce separately.

Gratinée aux Poires, Sabayon au Stilton
(Gratin of Pears, Stilton Sabayon)

Gratin of Pears

1/3 cup lemon juice

1/2 cup white wine

2 red apples, peeled, cored and thinly sliced

2 Bartlett pears, peeled, cored and thinly sliced

1/2 cup walnuts, chopped

In a medium nonreactive saucepan over low heat, combine lemon juice and wine. Bring to a simmer. Poach fruit until soft and tender, about 8 minutes. Do not overcook. Drain and set aside.

Stilton Sabayon

1/2 cup white wine

2 egg yolks

1/2 cup Stilton cheese, crumbled

In a small bowl combine wine and egg yolks, whisk until frothy. Put in a double boiler, stirring over simmering water until thick and glossy, about 3 minutes. Remove from heat and add cheese. Mix well and reserve.

Preheat broiler. In an oval gratin dish, arrange fruit and sprinkle with walnuts. Pour the Sabayon over and place under the broiler. Cook until set and well-browned (do not let it burn). Serve immediately.

Mark Monette
Flagstaff House

Flagstaff House, one of Colorado's most scenic restaurants, overlooks Boulder and imparts to its visitors the beauty and spirit of the mountains.

In 1929, Hattie Belchert built a summer cottage on this 6,000-square-foot mountain site. Years later, Hugo Buelk purchased the property, converted it into a summer restaurant and named it Flagstaff House. In 1971, Don Monette opened it as an all-year eating establishment, after renovating and expanding the property. His son, Mark, has been executive chef since 1985.

Mark says his "love of food and wine" inspired him to become a chef. He states he was "raised at Flagstaff House, mainly in the dining room." That was in the late seventies and early eighties when great changes in food awareness made such an impact on this country, with California the leader. "I was part of all this from the beginning," says Mark. "It was an exciting time, still is, and is getting more so every year."

Mark went to the Napa Valley for a short time after high school to learn about food and wine. His next stop was New York City, where he worked for three years in some of the top French restaurants: La Réserve, the Quilted Giraffe, the Water Club and Restaurant Raphael.

He then left for France and worked briefly for restaurateur Alain Nonnet, in Issoudun in the Loire Valley. Mr. Nonnet, in turn, recommended him to his friend, Chef Jean Deligne of the world-famous restaurant Taillevent in Paris. Mark was accepted for an apprenticeship. Though it was an incredible learning experience, the kitchen atmosphere was intense. Every cook, saucier and sous-chef was unyieldingly serious. No one would dare to touch a utensil that belonged to someone else for fear of being yelled at. Everything had to be perfect or one could expect to hear about it.

Despite the severe atmosphere, the job had its lighter moments. Mark recalls an incident which happened in the kitchen late one evening. Chef Deligne had an extra soufflé. Mark was standing in a corner when Deligne called him over and gave him the soufflé to eat. Every eye in the kitchen was fixed on Mark, for no one had seen the chef do such a thing. Mark hesitated but, he ate it.

From Taillevent, he worked briefly for the Troisgros brothers in Roanne.

When the chef at Flagstaff House retired, it was a perfect opportunity for Mark to return to Boulder and take over the operation of the kitchen.

One sees the influence of Mark's French training in the impressive decor of the restaurant: enormous arrangements of fresh flowers, exquisite Villeroy-Boch and Fitz Floyd China, as well as in the preparation and presentation of the food. Still Mark labels the cuisine at Flagstaff House "innovative American." He uses many French techniques, but also borrows from the Orient, where he has visited and taken cooking classes in Singapore and Hong Kong. He doesn't use heavy cream or butter but instead flavorful and healthy olive oil, broth and light concoctions.

The Flagstaff House is distinguished for more than its food. Gary Cummins, the head sommelier, proudly proclaims that every year since 1983 the restaurant has received the Grand Award from **Wine Spectator** magazine for having one of the top wine lists in the world.

Menu for Six

Flan of Lobster and Scallops with Two Caviars

Ahi Tuna in Mustard Crust with Red Pepper Nage

Tenderloin of Lamb with Sweet Peppers en Strudel

Coconut Tart with Piña Colada Ice Cream

Wine Recommendations

1989 Chablis Premier Cru Vaillons, Dauvissat

1990 Sauvignon Blanc, Buena Vista, Lake County

1985 Chianti Classico, Ruffino Riserva Ducale

"This menu is a perfect spring menu which my guests will enjoy because it will not leave a person feeling heavy. It uses all natural ingredients."
—Mark Monette

Serves 6

1 cup heavy cream

1 cup milk

5 eggs

Pinch nutmeg

Pinch saffron

1/2 tsp. garlic, minced

1 sprig tarragon, chopped

Pinch cayenne pepper

Salt and pepper to taste

6 deep sea scallops

1 8-ounce lobster tail, cooked and diced

1 can each, black and golden Romanoff caviar
   (available at specialty food stores)

6 3/4 cup ramekins, oiled

Preheat oven to 375°F.

In a medium-size bowl, mix together the first 8 ingredients. Season with salt and pepper. Let stand 5 minutes, then strain custard.

Slice each scallop into 3 pieces. Place 1 scallop in bottom of each ramekin. Divide diced lobster among ramekins and place over scallops. Pour custard over and bake for 25 to 30 minutes.

Unmold and serve garnished with some black and some golden caviar on the side of the plate.

Ahi Tuna in Mustard Crust with Red Pepper Nage

Serves 6

Tuna

3 8-ounce slices of sushi tuna (in the shape of small logs)

2 Tbsp. Dijon mustard

3/4 cup bread crumbs seasoned with:

1/4 tsp. ground cumin

1/4 tsp. whole mustard seeds

3 small cloves garlic, minced

6 sprigs fresh thyme, shredded

Pinch of cayenne pepper

Salt and pepper to taste

3 Tbsp. canola oil

Brush tuna with Dijon mustard and roll in seasoned bread crumbs. In a large skillet over medium-high heat, warm 3 Tbsp. canola oil. Sauté tuna until golden brown all around the log, about 8 to 10 minutes in all (tuna should be left rare in center).

Red Pepper Nage

6 ounces (1 1/2 sticks) unsalted butter

3 red bell peppers, seeded and chopped

1 cup dry Vermouth

3 cups fish stock (see Madeleine's Pantry)

6 sprigs fresh thyme

Pinch of dried fennel seeds

Fresh black pepper to taste

1 bay leaf

In a medium-size pan over low heat, melt 2 Tbsp. of butter. Sauté red peppers, stirring for 4 minutes. Raise heat to medium-high. Add dry Vermouth and reduce by 1/2. Lower heat to moderate. Add remaining ingredients and simmer, uncovered for 20 minutes. Remove from heat. Remove and discard bay leaf. Strain the solids, reserving the liquids and purée the solids in blender or processor. Return to liquids and heat again. Blend in remaining butter, little by little. Season with salt and pepper.

Presentation: Place several tablespoons of Red Pepper Nage Sauce on individual plates. Slice tuna and place on top of Nage Sauce. Serve immediately.

Serves 6

2 1-lb. tenderloins of lamb

Salt and pepper to taste

3 sprigs fresh rosemary, chopped

3 sprigs fresh thyme, shredded

10 fresh sage leaves, chopped

2 cloves garlic, minced

3 Tbsp. olive oil

2 red bell peppers, seeded, julienned

2 gold bell peppers, seeded, julienned

6 sheets filo dough (see Madeleine's Pantry)

1/4 cup butter, melted

Lightly season tenderloins of lamb with salt and pepper.

Combine chopped herbs with minced garlic. Rub 1/2 of the mixture over the 2 tenderloins of lamb. Reserve remaining herb mixture.

In a large skillet over high heat, heat the olive oil. Add lamb and quickly sear on both sides. Remove from pan and cool. Set aside.

Sauté peppers in the same pan, stirring until wilted. Season with salt and pepper. Remove from pan and cool.

Preheat oven to 400°F.

Brush one filo sheet with some melted butter and put another sheet of filo dough on top. Repeat procedure until 3 filo sheets have been used. (Repeat this for the second tenderloin of lamb.) Extra filo dough may be refrozen.

Place each cold tenderloin of lamb on the prepared filo dough. Divide remaining herbs and garlic mixture and half of the pepper mixture among the 2 tenderloins of lamb and place on top of each one. Roll filo dough around lamb.

Bake lamb for 10 to 12 minutes. Do not overcook, lamb should be served pink.

Presentation: Slice lamb and place on warm plates. Serve with remaining peppers on the side.

Coconut Tart with Piña Colada Ice Cream

Serves 8 to 10

Tart Shell
Makes 1 11-inch tart

1/2 cup butter, room temperature

1/4 cup sugar

1/2 cup almonds, ground

2 Tbsp. marzipan or almond paste

1 large egg yolk

1 1/4 cups flour

11-inch tart pan with removable fluted rim

In a bowl with an electric mixer, cream butter, sugar, ground almonds and marzipan or almond paste. Mix in egg yolk. Remove bowl from mixer and stir in flour. It will be soft, pliable dough. Press evenly into tart shell with fingers. Mold edges first then cover bottom of pan. Chill for 45 minutes.

Coconut Filling

1 cup shredded coconut

1/2 cup sugar

2 eggs

1 cup whole milk

Preheat oven to 350°F. Combine all ingredients in bowl and mix well. Pour into chilled tart shell. Bake for 25 minutes or until filling is set and shell is lightly browned on edges. Cool on rack.

Chocolate Ganache

4 ounces semi-sweet chocolate

1/2 cup heavy cream

Cut chocolate into small shavings. Place in small bowl. Heat cream to boiling and pour over chocolate. Stir until well blended.

Smooth the ganache over the top of the cooled, baked tart.

Piña Colada Ice Cream
Makes about 1 quart

1 cup heavy cream

2 cups milk

5/8 cup sugar

5 egg yolks

1/4 cup pineapple juice

1/4 cup canned coconut milk

1 ounce (2 Tbsp.) dark rum

In a mixing bowl, whisk together heavy cream, milk, sugar and egg yolks. Transfer to a saucepan. Over medium heat bring mixture to a boil, stirring constantly. Remove from heat and strain. Chill thoroughly.

Add pineapple juice, coconut milk and dark rum. Pour this mixture into an ice cream machine and churn, according to the manufacturer's instructions, until frozen. Serve with Coconut Tart.

Dave Query
Cliff Young's

It was not so much the ambition to be a chef as it was a desire to work in different places that prompted Dave Query to enter the culinary world.

As a fourteen-year old boy in Boulder, he first presided at the Mustard Stand, a hot dog and hamburger place where "you either loved the work or hated it." He loved it. After working in a few other restaurants, Dave was accepted at the Culinary Institute in Hyde Park, New York.

During its twenty-one month program each student at the Institute is required to do an externship. Dave was assigned to serve for five months as chef on the 150-foot yacht of Malcolm Forbes. The former chef had just been fired, so Dave assumed all the duties of the kitchen. What a responsibility for a young man! It meant supervising corporate parties several times a week and entertaining dignitaries, royalty and celebrities, including President Reagan, Prince Charles of Great Britain, Andy Warhol, the Rolling Stones and Imelda Marcos. Every night brought aboard a "Who's Who" of the world. Needless to say, it was fascinating.

After graduation from the Institute in 1985, Dave moved to Glencoe, Illinois, to open a restaurant for his uncle. Afterwards, Dave took a position as chef at the Blue Mesa Restaurant in downtown Chicago.

Dave's wife, Amy, graduated from the Culinary Institute in June, 1986. The couple went to work as cooks for a year at the exclusive Crystal Downs Country Club, located west of Traverse City, Michigan.

The club's beautiful golf course was designed by Allister MacKinze of Pebble Beach golf course fame. During their stay at Crystal Downs, Dave and Amy were asked to assume the roles of general manager and chef. They accepted and for the next three summers alternated roles. The arrangement worked nicely. It let them learn both positions and offered variety, larger salaries, and the chance to travel during the off-season from September to May.

The first year they went to California. Amy worked as chef at the Mesa Café on the border between Berkeley and Oakland. She had done her externship there when a student at the Institute. Dave, on the other hand, went from restaurant to restaurant working without pay. He simply found being in kitchens of famous eateries such as Chez Panisse, Zuni, Santa Fe Bar and Grill, Stars and Campton Place an exhilarating experience.

The next off-season Dave and Amy left for France. For five months they walked the country carrying backpacks. They went through the east, down the coast, then back to Paris.

For their third year of off-time travel, they chose New Orleans, Amy's hometown and the city where they were married. They worked in a restaurant owned by a friend as day and night sous-chefs, positions which allowed them to experiment with the unique style of Louisiana culinary techniques.

After a last summer in Michigan, they returned to Boulder in 1989. Dave bought the Lickskillet Café which he sold in 1990. A month later, he was hired as chef at one of Denver's most elegant restaurants, Cliff Young's. This eatery, where everything and everyone, from the setting to the well-trained staff, conspires towards beauty, is a perfect place for Dave's creativity. It shows. Each plate comes to the table looking like a work of art, and each bite is a taste of strong, clear flavors. But the chef's talent does not stop with the entrées. It extends to his desserts which are dazzlingly beautiful and in a class by themselves. No one can match his exquisite tuile served with ginger crème anglaise, fresh fruits and Grand Marnier truffles.

Menu for Four

Summer Gazpacho with Avocado and Grilled Shrimp

Jalapeño Corn Fritters

Filet Mignon of Tuna with Sweet Soy and Ginger Butter Sauce

Onion Biscuits

Cantaloupe with Minted Yogurt Sauce

Wine Recommendations

Manzanilla Sherry "La Gitana," Hildalgo

*1988 Chardonnay, Cambria Reserve,
Santa Maria*

"This is a light summer menu which features dishes very popular at Cliff Young's restaurant. The Gazpacho and dessert may be prepared a day ahead. The tuna should be very fresh. Bon appétit!" —Dave Query

Serves 4

7 to 8 large tomatoes to make 3 cups purée

6 Tbsp. each: red onion, green onion, zucchini, cucumber,
    yellow squash, cantaloupe and roasted yellow pepper*,
    finely chopped

1 Tbsp. minced garlic

2 Tbsp. minced pitted Greek olives

1 Tbsp. balsamic vinegar

Tabasco Sauce, to taste

Worchestershire Sauce, to taste

Salt and pepper to taste

1 ripe avocado, sliced

4 large shrimp, peeled, deveined and grilled

2 Tbsp. quality olive oil

Sprigs of cilantro for garnish

*See Madeleine's Pantry

Skin and core tomatoes. Purée in food processor. Strain. Add finely chopped vegetables, garlic, Greek olives, balsamic vinegar, Tabasco and Worchestershire Sauce to purée. Season with salt and pepper to taste. Refrigerate 24 hours.

Presentation: Pour soup into cold soup plates and top with a slice of avocado, grilled shrimp and a thin swirl of quality olive oil. Garnish with a sprig of cilantro. Serve.

Jalapeño Corn Fritters

Makes 16 fritters

3 to 5 jalapeño peppers to make 3 Tbsp. chopped

1 cup yellow cornmeal

3/4 cup all purpose flour

1 Tbsp. sugar

1 tsp. baking powder

1/2 tsp. salt

1 cup buttermilk

1 egg, beaten

1 Tbsp. minced pimento

1 Tbsp. minced parsley

1 quart peanut oil

Char jalapeño peppers under broiler (see Madeleine's Pantry). Peel, seed and chop finely.

Mix cornmeal, flour, sugar, baking powder and salt together. Add buttermilk and beaten egg. Mix thoroughly. Add jalapeño pepper, pimento and parsley. Form into a ball and refrigerate for 30 minutes.

Heat peanut oil in a heavy pan until it reaches 350°F. Using two teaspoons, shape fritters by exchanging a full teaspoon of fritter mixture from spoon to spoon. When mixture has shaped into a football shape, drop quickly and carefully into hot oil. Cook 2 to 3 minutes or until golden brown. Drain on paper toweling.

Delicious served with Summer Gazpacho.

Filet Mignon of Tuna with Sweet Soy and Ginger Butter Sauce

Serves 4

4 8-ounce fresh tuna fillets

1/4 cup Sherry

2 1/2 Tbsp. sesame oil

2 1/2 Tbsp. soy sauce

1 green onion, finely chopped

1 Tbsp. grated orange zest

1/2 cup white wine

Juice of 1/2 lemon, strained

1 1/2 sticks (6 ounces) unsalted butter, diced

1 Tbsp. minced fresh ginger

8 Tbsp. sweet soy sauce

    (available at Oriental markets)

Mix Sherry, sesame oil, soy sauce, green onion and orange zest together and pour them over the tuna portions. Marinate for 30 minutes, turning frequently.

In a nonreactive saucepan, over medium heat, reduce white wine and lemon juice to 2 tablespoons of liquid. Remove from heat and slowly add butter, piece by piece. Place pan over low heat occasionally during this process to keep a constant heat, but do not let mixture boil. After all butter has been incorporated, add ginger and remove from heat.

Keep the sauce in a warm place until needed (may be kept in a thermos for 1 hour). Preheat broiler.

Grill tuna for 4 to 5 minutes on each side. Do not overcook.

Presentation: Place tuna on a warm plate. Pour Ginger Butter Sauce over it and drizzle about 2 tablespoons (or to taste) of sweet soy sauce through the butter sauce on each plate. Serve at once.

Onion Biscuits

Makes 1 1/2 dozen

1/2 medium onion, minced

2 cloves garlic, minced

1 Tbsp. butter

4 cups all purpose flour, sifted

2 tsp. salt

2 Tbsp. baking powder

1 1/2 sticks (6 ounces) unsalted butter, diced

1 1/2 cups milk

Preheat oven to 375°F.

Sauté onion and garlic in butter for 3 to 4 minutes. Cool. In a medium bowl, blend flour, salt and baking powder. Add butter and cut into the dry ingredients with a pastry blender until the mixture is the consistency of coarse cornmeal. Add sautéed onion and garlic and mix. Make a well in the center and pour in all of the milk at once. Stir well.

Turn the dough onto a lightly-floured board. Knead the dough gently and quickly for 1/2 minute. Roll the dough with a lightly-floured rolling pin to 1/2-inch thickness. Cut the dough in typical rounds with a 2-inch biscuit cutter that has been lightly dipped in flour. Place biscuits on an ungreased baking sheet and bake for 12 to 15 minutes, until done. Serve warm.

Serves 4

1 cantaloupe, rind removed and sliced
1 cup plain nonfat yogurt
1/2 Tbsp. honey
1 Tbsp. fresh mint, finely chopped
Mint springs for garnish

Mix yogurt and honey together. Add chopped fresh mint. Pour sauce over sliced cantaloupe. Garnish with mint sprigs.

Mo Riasati
Saffron

While he was a student at the University of Colorado at Denver, Mo Riasati needed a job to help pay his tuition, so he decided to take a part-time job cooking at the former London House Restaurant. He loved it and stayed there through his university years.

After college, he went to the Canterbury Inn Restaurant, where they put him in charge of the night shift, an important move in this popular eatery. It was then that Mo decided to make his mark as a chef. He felt that "patrons in many restaurants were given foods nicely served, but absolutely tasteless." He slowly introduced some specialty spices, such as saffron, that were old in origin and widely used in the cooking of Mo's native Iran.

Mo's dream was to open a small restaurant. Several years ago, he and a partner, Faye Samimi, opened a sandwich shop. When the space next door to their shop became vacant, they took it over, expanded it into a full eating establishment and upgraded the menu. Their small, elegant restaurant, Saffron, is the twin of the best eatery in Tehran, Iran, Farid, which Faye Samimi's husband successfully managed before coming to the United States.

In his cooking, Mo knows how to play with spices, combining them in proper balance. His food is not only good, but also reasonably priced. To insure this, he intends to keep preparing alone every step of both lunch and dinner until he finds someone who can do the work exactly the way he does it.

175

Salad Shiraz

Chicken Saffron

Rolet (Cake Roll with Strawberry Cream Filling)

Wine Recommendations

1990 Dry Chenin Blanc, Martin Brothers, Paso Robles

1989 Okfener Bockstein Riesling Kabinett,
Dr. Fischer, Mosel-Saar-Ruwer

"Saffron is an aromatic spice that can be used to give any food an exciting taste. The recipes included are some of the most popular ones at Saffron Restaurant. They are easy to prepare for both casual and elegant dining." —Mo Riasati

Salad Shiraz

Serves 4

2 ripe tomatoes, peeled and seeded

3 medium cucumbers

2 Tbsp. fresh mint, chopped

7 Tbsp. olive oil

1 1/2 Tbsp. fresh lime juice

Salt and pepper to taste

4 lettuce leaves

Dice the tomatoes. Peel and seed the cucumbers and dice. Combine the first 6 ingredients. Chill. Serve on lettuce leaves.

Chicken Saffron

Serves 4

4 chicken breast halves, boned and skinned

1/2 cup plain yogurt

2 garlic cloves, minced

Pinch of salt

Dash of pepper

1 tsp. fresh lemon juice

1 small onion, chopped

3 Tbsp. olive oil

2 cups dry white wine

Pinch of saffron

1 Tbsp. basil, chopped

1 Tbsp. parsley, chopped

1/2 lb. fresh spinach, chopped

2 tomatoes, peeled and diced

1/2 cup heavy cream

Cut chicken breasts into 1-inch wide strips or chunks and place in a nonreactive bowl. Combine yogurt, 1/2 the garlic, salt, pepper and 1/2 tsp. lemon juice. Pour yogurt marinade over the chicken, mixing gently so all the chicken is coated with the yogurt mixture. Refrigerate for 4 hours.

In a heavy skillet, cook the onion in olive oil over moderately high heat, stirring, until browned. Add chicken and cook for 3 minutes. Add white wine and reduce by half. Add remaining 1/2 tsp. lemon juice, saffron, basil, parsley and spinach and cook over moderate heat, stirring occasionally, for 4 to 5 minutes. Add heavy cream and warm through. Serve with rice.

Rolet (Cake Roll with Strawberry Cream Filling)

Serves 8 to 10

Cake

7 eggs separated, at room temperature

7 Tbsp. sugar

1/2 tsp. vanilla

7 Tbsp. flour, sifted

2 Tbsp. safflower oil

Confectioner's sugar

Preheat oven to 375°F. Butter a 11x16x1-inch rimmed cookie sheet. Cover with waxed paper and butter the paper.

In a medium-size bowl, beat the egg yolks with sugar and vanilla to a light, creamy consistency, about 7 minutes. Add flour gradually and mix. Add oil and blend well.

In another bowl, beat the egg whites until they hold stiff peaks. Fold the egg whites gently but thoroughly into the yolk mixture. Pour the batter into the prepared pan and spread it evenly with a rubber spatula. Bake the cake for 15 minutes or until golden brown on top. Remove from the oven and cover with a cloth that has been wrung out in cold water. Cool cake and let sit for 1 hour.

Remove cloth, loosen cake edges from the cookie sheet with a spatula and dust top with confectioner's sugar. Turn out on waxed paper and carefully peel paper off. Let cool completely.

Filling

2 cups heavy cream
3 Tbsp. powdered sugar
10 strawberries, stemmed and sliced
Additional powdered sugar for garnish

Whip cream until stiff. Add sugar and blend well. Spread the whipped cream evenly on the cake and lay strawberry slices on top. Roll up like a jellyroll and dust with powdered sugar. Refrigerate until ready to serve.

Cake may be prepared several hours ahead.

Madeleine St. John
La Bonne Cuisine Cooking School

As a teenager growing up in German-occupied Belgium, Madeleine Launoy had little opportunity to develop her culinary skills. A stint in the Belgian underground and wartime shortages of sugar, flour, butter and spices did not a pantry make. For Madeleine, learning to cook was of secondary importance.

Madeleine came to America in 1947 to finish her college education. There she met and married her husband, Bill St. John, then a young dentist. Neither of them knew very much about cooking. Madeleine began her stove-side career literally from "scratch."

The St. Johns moved to Denver in 1949 and began what was to become a large family of nine children - and ample opportunity to cook. On a trip to Provence, France twelve years ago, Madeleine met Simca Beck, co-author with Julia Child of **Mastering the Art of French Cooking,** *who encouraged Madeleine to broaden her burgeoning culinary talent.*

Madeleine studied with Simca Beck in her home in France and has returned to Europe every year since then to enroll in a different cooking school. She has taken classes in Paris, at Princesse Marie-Blanche de

Broglie and La Varenne; at l'Oustau de Baumanière in Les Baux-en-Provence, France; in London, at The Cordon Bleu; in Hintelshan, England, at Robert Carrier Seminar of Cooking; in Cork, Ireland, at Ballymaloe Cookery School; and in Madrid, at Alicia Rios Ivars' Cooking School.

She has worked in the kitchens of L'Auberge de Reillanne in Reillanne, France; Restaurante El Cenador, Restaurante Juan de Alzate and Restaurante Cabo Major in Madrid. She has participated in cooking demonstrations by chefs such as Jean-Paul Duquesnoy, owner of Duquesnoy, and Jean Deligne of Restaurant Taillevent, both in Paris. For twelve years, she has run her own cookery school in Denver, La Bonne Cuisine.

A Dinner For Special Friends, Menu for Six

Wild Mushroom Consommé

Tenderloin of Beef with Sauce Poivrade

Julienne of Carrots

Mixed Green Salad with French Dressing

Linzer Torte

Chocolate Truffles

Wine Recommendations

Rainwater Madeira

1987 Chateau Calon-Segur, St-Estephe

1979 Smith-Woodhouse, Late Bottled Vintage Porto

"For my husband and me, having friends for dinner is one of our more pleasurable and satisfying endeavors. An evening of good food and wine attractively presented and shared with close friends is a true communion."
—Madeleine St. John

Serves 6

3 cups beef stock (see Madeleine's Pantry)
4 Tbsp. (1/2 stick), unsalted butter
12 large shitake mushrooms, chopped
6 scallions, cut into 2-inch lengths, finely julienned
Salt and pepper to taste

Heat broth to a simmer.

In a large skillet over moderate-high heat, melt butter and sauté mushrooms quickly, stirring, until just soft. Remove to platter. In same pan, lightly sauté scallions.

Add mushrooms and scallions to broth. Season with salt and pepper to taste. Serve very hot.

Tenderloin of Beef with Sauce Poivrade
(Peppered Brown Sauce)

Serves 6

Beef

1 4-lb. tenderloin of beef

1 1/2 cups red wine

1/3 cup tarragon wine vinegar

2 Tbsp. brandy

1 medium yellow onion, thinly sliced

3/4 tsp. dried tarragon

3/4 tsp. dried thyme

1 bay leaf, crumbled

2 Tbsp. butter, softened

Put the tenderloin of beef in a shallow nonreactive baking dish and sprinkle it with a little salt.

Combine the wine, tarragon vinegar, brandy, onion, tarragon, thyme and bay leaf. Pour the marinade over the beef, cover it tightly with foil and refrigerate it for 3 days, turning the meat several times each day.

Preheat oven to 400°F.

Bring beef out of refrigerator 45 minutes to 1 hour before cooking it. Remove the beef from marinade and pat it dry with paper towels. Strain the marinade and reserve 1/2 cup for Sauce Poivrade.

Rub the beef with softened butter, and roast uncovered for 35 to 40 minutes for rare beef (your meat thermometer should read 120°).

Remove beef to a heated platter, cover and keep warm. The meat should stand covered for 20 minutes so that the meat tissues reabsorb their juices before carving.

Sauce Poivrade

1/4 cup olive oil

1/2 cup carrots, chopped

1/2 cup yellow onion, chopped

Bouquet garni (bay leaf, 6 sprigs parsley, 3 sprigs thyme)

1/4 cup tarragon wine vinegar

1 1/2 cups brown sauce (recipe follows)

6 peppercorns, crushed

2 Tbsp. butter

Salt to taste

Heat olive oil in a skillet, over moderate-high heat. Sauté carrots and onion with bouquet garni, stirring frequently, until onions are golden.

Drain off the oil and add the reserved marinade and tarragon wine vinegar. Cook the mixture, stirring constantly until it is reduced to 1/3. Add the brown sauce and simmer the sauce for 30 minutes.

Add crushed peppercorns and simmer the mixture for 10 minutes longer. Strain it through a fine sieve. Sauce may be prepared up to 2 hours ahead. Return the sauce to the heat, bring it to a boil, and add salt.

Before serving, stir in the softened butter.

Brown Sauce
Makes about 2 cups

6 Tbsp. clarified butter (see Madeleine's Pantry)

1/3 cup carrot, finely chopped

1/3 cup onion, finely chopped

1/3 cup celery, finely chopped

1/2 cup lean bacon, chopped

4 Tbsp. flour

6 cups beef stock (see Madeleine's Pantry)

2 tbsp. tomato paste

8 peppercorns

1/2 small bunch parsley

1 bay leaf

Salt and pepper to taste

In a heavy 2-quart saucepan over moderate heat, melt clarified butter. Cook the vegetables and bacon for 15 minutes, stirring occasionally. Stir in the flour and cook slowly for 10 minutes or until the flour browns.

Remove from the heat, pour in the hot beef stock and blend with a wire whisk. Stir in the tomato paste, peppercorns, parsley and bay leaf.

Turn heat to simmer and cook uncovered for 2 hours. Season with salt and pepper to taste. Strain, discarding the solids. Cool and refrigerate. Next day, remove fat from the top of sauce. (Sauce is ready to be used or can be frozen.)

Presentation: Carve tenderloin of beef into thin slices. Spoon some Sauce Poivrade over the slices and pass the remainder into a heated sauceboat.

Julienne of Carrots

Serves 6

2 lbs. carrots, peeled, julienned
Salt and pepper to taste

Steam julienned carrots for a few minutes. Season with salt and pepper.

Serves 6

Salad

Choose an assortment of greens:
> **1 each red leaf lettuce, mâche, Belgian endive, frisée**
1 bunch of radishes, thinly sliced
3 sprigs fresh marjoram, chopped
1 head bibb lettuce
1/3 cup parsley, minced
French Dressing (recipe follows)

Wash greens and dry well. Tear in bite-size pieces except bibb lettuce. Place in large bowl. Add radishes and marjoram. Lightly mix with some French Dressing.

Presentation: Place one leaf of bibb lettuce on each chilled salad plate. Lay mixed salad greens over. Sprinkle with minced parsley and serve.

French Dressing
Makes about 2/3 cup

8 Tbsp. virgin olive oil
2 Tbsp. red wine vinegar
1 tsp. salt
1 tsp. Dijon mustard
Pinch of sugar
1 tsp. lemon juice

Put all ingredients in a jar with a screw top. Shake well. Refrigerate. This vinaigrette recipe may be doubled.

Serves 6 to 8

Torte
Makes 1 9-inch torte

There are many variations of Linzer Torte. It can be made with strawberry or apricot jam or red currant jelly. The following version has been a favorite for over 30 years at the Cordon Bleu Cooking School in London. Linzer Torte should cool to room temperature before being served and should be eaten within two days. It can be frozen successfully after baking and cooling.

1 1/2 cups fresh raspberries

1 Tbsp. water

Raspberry jam to taste

1 cup all-purpose flour, sifted

1/4 tsp. salt

1 tsp. cinnamon

1 tsp. instant granulated coffee

8 Tbsp. butter

1/2 cup sugar

1 whole egg

1/2 tsp. grated lemon zest

2 1/2-ounces almonds, ground

In a saucepan over moderate heat, bring raspberries and water to a boil and cook rapidly for 2 to 3 minutes. Add raspberry jam to sweeten. Cool.

In a large mixing bowl, sift flour with the salt, cinnamon and coffee. Make a well in the center and into it put the butter, sugar, egg, lemon zest and almonds. Work ingredients together, form into a ball. Refrigerate, wrapped in waxed paper, for at least 1/2 hour.

Preheat oven to 375°F.

On a floured board, roll out half the pastry to 1/4 to 1/2-inch thick, keeping the other half refrigerated.

Line a 9-inch butter flan ring with the pastry, and roll the pin across the top of the ring to cut off excess dough. Fill the ring with the cold raspberry mixture.

Roll out remaining pastry, cut into strips, and arrange in a lattice top over the filling.

Bake in oven for 20 to 30 minutes or until pastry is lightly browned. Cool torte a little. Brush entire surface of torte with warm Quick Red Currant Jelly Glaze.

Quick Red Currant Jelly Glaze

1/2 cup red currant jelly
2 Tbsp. sugar

Stir red currant jelly with sugar over moderately high heat for 2 to 3 minutes until thick enough to coat a wooden spoon with a light film.

Chocolate Truffles

This is my mother's recipe for truffles. They freeze beautifully and make lovely gifts.

Makes about 30 truffles

1/2 lb. (2 sticks) butter, softened

3/4 lb. imported European chocolate, melted *

1/4 tsp. vanilla extract

2 egg yolks

6 Tbsp. powdered sugar

Powdered chocolate

> * I use Callebaut bittersweet chocolate, available at specialty food stores.

Mix well together butter, chocolate, vanilla extract, egg yolks and powdered sugar. Pour in a flat container such as a pie plate. Let cool in refrigerator. Cut in pieces and form into small balls. Roll in powdered chocolate. (I use a mixture of Hershey's cocoa and instant chocolate flavored drink mix.) Store in airtight container. Use waxed paper to separate layers of truffles. Refrigerate or freeze.

Peter St. John
O Sole Mio

"*I grew up in restaurants. My parents owned five of them in Munich and I started helping in the kitchen when I was four years old,*" *says Peter St. John.* "*I watched the chefs working and became fascinated and amazed by their work. I thought, this is what I want to do someday.*"

Peter's mother taught him how to cook and when he turned fourteen he held his first apprenticeship in his hometown at the world-renowned Bavarian Court Hotel. After several other apprenticeships in Munich under the supervision of Michelin two- and three-star chefs, he embarked on a ten year "journeymanship." This entailed moving from restaurant to restaurant every six months, working in each one as an assistant to the chef and assuming greater responsibility with each assignment. Peter feels that these experiences enabled him to perfect his skill in the art of cooking.

From Germany, he traveled to the Bahamas where he became the private chef to the United States ambassador. Peter always wanted to come to America and the Ambassador eventually helped him realize his dream. He arrived in Miami in 1983 to take a position as executive sous-chef at the Miami Lakes Country Club, the residence of the Miami Dolphins football team before each home game. After he had been there for three weeks, the chef was transferred and Peter was asked to assume full responsibility as chef of the country club's dining facility.

From Miami, he moved to Fort Lauderdale to become the chef at a five-star French restaurant, Petit Bon.

After one and a half years, he was offered a sous-chef position at Café Max in Pompano Beach. He liked the New American free-style cuisine the café featured but realized that he could greatly improve its method of cooking, especially in the preparation of sauces.

After a couple of months, the owner opened a Café Max in Miami and Peter was asked to become the chef. Within three years, four similar eateries opened: Max's Place, Café Max, Max Luma and Max's Grill. Peter became their corporate chef, overseeing the entire operation. After a while, he felt it was time to move on. He went to Dallas as chef at the beautiful rooftop restaurant of the Sheraton Park Central. Within six months, the restaurant received a five-star rating.

Peter returned briefly to the Carribean before coming to Denver as the chef at the Palace Arms restaurant at the Brown Palace Hotel. One and a half years later, he and his principal partner, Mario Mazzei, purchased the building where O Sole Mio now stands.

Peter calls the cuisine of O Sole Mio "modern Italian." He does some traditional dishes and updates some others, but especially enjoys what he terms "off-the-wall and exciting food."

Chef St. John and his staff spent three weeks in Italy in August, 1991, visiting Calabria, Tuscany, Sicily, Umbria, and Rome, wining and dining along the way and gathering new culinary ideas.

Fall Dinner Menu for Six

Chestnut Soup with Apple Grappa Cream

Malfatti Ricotta Spinach Dumplings with Fennel Sausage
and Sage Cream

Flourless Chocolate, Pinenut and White Chocolate Chip Cake

Wine Recommendations

Amontillado Sherry, Emilio Lustau

1989 Dolcetto d'Alba, Bruno Giacosa

Peter contributes the following menu to the **Friends for Dinner** *cookbook and says: "This menu is perfect for a fall dinner. All the dishes, with the exception of the Sage Cream, may be prepared in advance, leaving the hostess time to enjoy her guests."* —Peter St. John

Serves 6

Soup

1 lb. fresh chestnuts

4 Tbsp. butter

1 small yellow onion, chopped

1 carrot, peeled and chopped

1 rib celery, chopped

1 leek (white part only), chopped

1/2 parsnip, chopped

3 cups chicken stock (see Madeleine's Pantry)

1 bay leaf

1/8 tsp. ground allspice

1 clove

Pinch ground cinnamon or to taste

1 Tbsp. lemon juice

1/4 tsp. dried thyme

1/4 tsp. dried oregano

Salt and pepper to taste

1/4 cup chives, finely chopped, for garnish

Preheat oven to 400°F.

Make a cross cut through the peel of the chestnut on the pointed end. Spread chestnuts on a cookie sheet and roast them for 7 minutes or until peel gets brittle. Peel chestnuts while still hot for easier peeling.

In a large pan over medium heat, melt butter. Sauté chopped vegetables, stirring occasionally, for 10 minutes. Add chicken stock. Bring soup to a boil. Skim foam which accumulates on the surface. Turn heat to simmer, add bay leaf, ground allspice, clove, cinnamon, lemon juice, thyme, oregano, salt and pepper and cook uncovered for 1 hour. Remove from heat and cool slightly.

Strain the solids, reserving the liquid. Purée the solids in a food processor or blender. Return the purée to the liquid. (If soup is too thick, thin with some extra chicken stock.) Correct seasonings. Serve in warmed soup plates garnished with chopped chives and Apple Grappa Cream.

Apple Grappa Cream

1/2 Granny Smith apple, peeled, cored and diced

1 Tbsp. grappa
    (available at liquor stores)

6 Tbsp. heavy cream

1/2 tsp. lemon juice

Sugar to taste

In a small saucepan over moderate heat, boil apple, grappa and cream for 5 minutes. Cool slightly. Purée in blender with lemon juice and sugar.

Malfatti Ricotta Spinach Dumplings with Fennel Sausage and Sage Cream

Makes 14-18, depending on size

Dumplings

4 tsp. butter

1/2 cup yellow onion, diced

2 tsp. garlic, finely chopped

1 1/2 lbs. spinach, blanched, squeezed dry and chopped

2 tsp. ground nutmeg

2 lbs. ricotta

5 large eggs

1/2 cup parsley, finely chopped

Salt and pepper to taste

In a sauté pan over moderate heat, warm butter. Sauté onion and garlic until translucent. Add spinach and nutmeg. Mix well and cool.

In a large bowl, mix ricotta with eggs. Add spinach mixture.

In a large pot, over medium-high heat, bring 2 quarts of salted water to a boil. Lower heat to simmer. Make dumplings with an ice cream scoop or large tablespoon and drop into simmering water. Cook for 7 minutes (when ready they will rise to the top of the water). Plunge dumplings into ice water and drain.

Cook only 3 or 4 dumplings at a time. Let water return to simmer before cooking a second batch of dumplings. Set aside and keep warm.

Fennel Sausage

3 tsp. roasted fennel seed

1 lb. ground pork

1 cup plus 1 Tbsp. ground salt pork

1/2 cup ice water

1 tsp. sweet paprika

1 tsp. dried mixed herbs (oregano, thyme and rosemary)

2 tsp. crushed red pepper

Salt and pepper to taste

Preheat oven to 350°F. Brown fennel seeds in sauté pan for 2 minutes, stirring constantly. Watch carefully as they brown quickly.

Combine all ingredients. Form sausage into 2-inch round balls. Place on a cookie sheet and roast for 10 minutes. Set aside

Sage Cream

1 cup dry white wine

3 bay leaves

1/2 cup sage stems

2 tsp. garlic, finely chopped

2 cups heavy cream

3 tsp. sage leaves, chopped

1 tsp. ground nutmeg

Salt and pepper to taste

In a saucepan over moderate heat, bring wine, bay leaves, sage stems and garlic to a boil. Reduce by 2/3. Strain. Return liquid to saucepan. Add heavy cream, chopped sage leaves, nutmeg, salt and pepper to taste. Bring to a boil but do not reduce.

Tomato Sauce

3 Tbsp. olive oil

1/2 cup yellow onion, finely diced

2 tsp. garlic, minced

10 Roma tomatoes, peeled, seeded and diced

Pinch of salt and sugar

Freshly ground pepper to taste

2 Tbsp. fresh basil, chopped

2 tsp. balsamic vinegar

2 cups grated Parmesan Reggiano

8 sprigs of sage

1/2 cup chopped chives

To assemble dish: In a saucepan over moderate heat, warm olive oil. Sauté onions until translucent. Add garlic and tomatoes. Season with salt, sugar and freshly ground pepper. Cook until most of the liquid has evaporated. Take off heat and add basil and vinegar.

To serve: Grill the roasted sausages until brown and slice each into 4 pieces. (You may grill the sausages in the pan or on a stovetop grill as well as on an outdoor grill.) Set aside and keep warm.

Preheat oven to 350°F. Place 3 dumplings in a bowl. Top with about 1/4 cup Sage Cream and one teaspoon Tomato Sauce on each dumpling. Sprinkle dumplings generously with Parmesan Reggiano cheese and bake for 7 minutes. Arrange some sausages with the dumplings, garnish with the sage sprigs and sprinkle with the chives. Serve immediately.

Flourless Chocolate, Pinenut and White Chocolate Chip Cake

Serves 12 to 14

Makes one 10-inch cake

3 Tbsp. lightly toasted pinenuts or pecans

5 Tbsp. chopped white chocolate (Lindt Swiss White
Chocolate or Tobler Narcisse)

6 extra large eggs, room temperature

1 1/3 cup sugar

1/2 cup water

12 ounces semi-sweet chocolate, chopped

8 ounces (2 sticks) sweet butter, room temperature

1 Tbsp. rum

Vanilla ice cream

Preheat oven to 325°F.

Line the bottom of a 10-inch cake pan with a piece of parchment. Spray paper and sides of pan with non-stick spray. Mix pinenuts or pecans with chopped white chocolate and sprinkle evenly over the bottom of the pan.

In a large bowl with an electric mixer, beat eggs with 1/3 cup of sugar until thick and pale.

In a small pan over moderate heat, combine water and remaining 1 cup sugar and bring to a boil. Remove from heat. Add semi-sweet chocolate and mix until well incorporated. Add butter and rum and mix well.

Stir chocolate mixture into egg mixture and combine well.

Pour batter into prepared cake pan. Set in pan of hot water and bake for 50 minutes or until set in the center.

Cool on wire rack to room temperature and invert onto a serving tray. Refrigerate for 2 hours or more.

Serve with vanilla ice cream.

Christian Schmidt
Scanticon Hotel and Conference Center

German-born Christian Schmidt literally grew up in the culinary world. His parents have both been life-long participants in hotel and restaurant industry. His father is still at work as a chef in a Berlin hotel. Christian began helping his father when he was eleven and by the age of fourteen knew that he, too, wanted a career as a chef.

From 1974 to 1978, Christian trained at the Kaiserhof Hotel near Strasbourg, then gained additional experience in several hotels throughout Germany, including one in Heidelberg, where he worked during its renowned asparagus season.

Christian believes that his greatest culinary experience took place when he was working in hotels around Karlsruhe and Baden Baden, an area more trendy than other parts of Germany. Because it is located near Alsace, it has been subject to French influence and an early revolution toward nouvelle cuisine. Old ways of preparing recipes changed radically. For Christian, his time there "was fun."

However, he decided to move to the United States in 1981 to look for better career opportunities. He thought he would enjoy living in Colorado. His mother resides in Denver and he had visited her several times. Christian found work as a line cook almost immediately at the then Fairmont Hotel. Several other employees in its kitchen were from Germany and Alsace so they helped Christian bridge the gap between his native German and English.

In three years, he became executive sous-chef and one year later was appointed night sous-chef for the elegant Marquis Room at the Fairmont. In 1985, four years after joining the Fairmont, he was asked to become the new Snowmass Conference Center's first executive chef. Soon after the grand opening for two thousand people, he was invited by the Brown Palace Hotel to be the chef at their private hotel club.

He returned to the Mile High City and three months later was promoted to the position of executive chef of the Brown Palace. He held this position for one and a half years and enjoyed it tremendously. He was particularly fond of the wine and food dinners that he hosted with Bill St. John, wine and dining critic for the **Rocky Mountain News**.

Then Christian moved on to the Grand Bay Hotel in Miami, Florida as their executive chef. This proved to be a turning point in his career. In this large hotel with two restaurants and a staff of forty-five cooks, he established his reputation nationally. He experimented with the many culinary trends unfolding at the time and learned more about the importance of diversity. In a short time, Christian and his staff elevated the Hotel to a Five-Star Mobil rating.

Despite his success at the Grand Bay Hotel, his heart and "mother and friends" were back in Denver. After a brief stay at Pebble Beach, California, where he helped Marvin Davis open the restaurant in his new hotel in Spanish Bay, he returned to Denver.

In 1988, a former co-worker from the Brown Palace who was working for Scanticon in Princeton, New Jersey, asked him to help open the Scanticon Hotel in Denver. He accepted and presides there today. His duties at the four-star Scandinavian-style hotel are to oversee the four restaurants, each with a distinctive cuisine, and the numerous banquets which the hotel hosts. One restaurant, the elegant Black Swan, recently won the prestigious Four Diamond award from the American Automobile Association.

Menu for Six

Chilled Strawberry Sorrel Soup

Seared Salmon

Mocha Mousse with Grand Marnier Vanilla Sauce

Wine Recommendation

1989 Dr. Burklin-Wolf Forster Jesuitengarten
Riesling Spatlese, Rheinpfalz

"This menu is perfect for those with a busy schedule who want a tasty and nutritious meal without a lot of preparation." —Christian Schmidt

Serves 6

4 cups strawberries

9 leaves fresh sorrel, finely chopped

1 cup dry white wine

2 Tbsp. honey

1 papaya, peeled and sliced

5 sorrel leaves, julienned

Clean, trim and slice strawberries. Put first four ingredients in bowl of processor and purée until smooth.

Chill the soup, covered, in refrigerator for several hours.

Serve in cold bowls, garnished with papaya slices and julienne of sorrel.

Serves 6

4 Tbsp. clarified butter (see Madeleine's Pantry)

6 4-ounce pieces of salmon fillet, skinned

3 Tbsp. light soy sauce

3 Tbsp. fresh lemon juice

1 Tbsp. butter

3 lbs. fresh spinach

White pepper to taste

1/4 cup crème fraîche *

1/4 cup salmon caviar *

*Available in most supermarkets or specialty food stores

In a large heavy sauté pan over medium-high heat, melt the clarified butter. Quickly sear salmon fillets until lightly browned, about 3 minutes on each side. Remove salmon from sauté pan and wipe fat out of pan.

Pour light soy sauce and lemon juice in pan. Return salmon to pan and cook for a few more minutes. Turn heat off.

Heat the butter in a large, heavy skillet or pan. Add the spinach. Cover at once and cook over high heat until steam appears. Reduce the heat and simmer until tender, about 4 to 5 minutes. Season with white pepper.

Presentation: Place salmon fillet on a warm plate and garnish with a dollop of crème fraîche. Mound some spinach in a corner of the plate and place a small amount of caviar on the opposite side.

Serve immediately.

Serves 8

Mocha Mousse

1/2 tsp. mocha extract

2 1/2 Tbsp. coffee liqueur

1/2 tsp. vanilla extract

2 cups heavy cream

2 egg whites

1/4 cup sugar

1 cup fresh raspberries

In a large bowl, mix together the mocha extract, coffee liqueur and vanilla extract.

In a small bowl with an electric mixer, whip heavy cream until stiff. In another bowl with electric mixer, whip egg whites until frothy; slowly add sugar and whip until stiff. Fold whipped cream into the coffee mixture and mix well. Fold in egg whites and mix well.

Divide mixture between 8 3/4-cup ramekins. Cover and freeze for several hours or overnight.

Presentation: When ready to serve, unmold on a dessert plate. Pour several tablespoons of Grand Marnier Vanilla Sauce over each Mocha Mouse and serve with fresh raspberries.

Grand Marnier Vanilla Sauce
Makes about 1 cup

3/4 cup milk

2 Tbsp. heavy cream

Dash salt

1/4 tsp. vanilla extract

2 tsp. cornstarch

1 egg yolk

2 Tbsp. sugar

2 Tbsp. Grand Marnier

Reserve 1 tablespoon of the milk. In a medium-size saucepan over medium heat, combine milk, heavy cream, salt and vanilla and bring to a boil. Mix cornstarch with the 1 Tbsp. milk and slowly add it to the boiling milk mixture. Cook for 2 minutes, stirring occasionally.

In a small bowl, whip together egg yolk, sugar and Grand Marnier until smooth.

Cool the milk mixture to room temperature. Add to the egg mixture and stir well. Chill, covered in refrigerator, for several hours.

Kevin Taylor
Zenith

Colorado native Kevin Taylor ventured into the culinary world at age fifteen and discovered that he loved the work. He apprenticed for five years at a country club in Denver under a young American chef and an older German cook who had worked at the Savoy Hotel in London for thirty years. He feels this taught him the best of both worlds: new techniques as well as classical cooking. Following another two-year stint at other country clubs, he worked for a summer at the legendary resort, the Greenbriar Hotel in White Sulphur Springs, West Virginia.

Determined from age nineteen to someday own his own restaurant, Kevin spent the next several years opening six different restaurants. This exposed him to all the problems associated with running an eating establishment.

Three years ago, at age twenty-five, Kevin Taylor and his partner Janet Wright opened Zenith. It soon became one of the top restaurants in Denver. Kevin attributes this success to his love of Colorado, understanding the eating habits of its people and to the use of regional and domestic ingredients such as goat cheese, Colorado trout and game. This produces the cuisine which Zenith has become known for, "Pure American Cooking."

This young, ambitious restaurateur, who believes "any great chef or cook is above all a great food chemist," will not wear a toque. He dons an apron and works behind the stove with his helpers, still learning, constantly working to improve Zenith's cuisine. He wants simpler and more composed offerings, reflecting a trend he sees in this country.

Menu for Six

**Lamb, Lentil and Artichoke Salad with
Rosemary Pepper Vinaigrette**

**Charbroiled Tuna with Black Bean "Chili",
Orange Crema and Mango Tomatillo Salsa**

Chocolate Bread Pudding with Chocolate Sauce

Wine Recommendations

Veuve Clicquot Rose Champagne

1989 Elk Cove Pinot Gris, Oregon

Porto Taylor-Fladgate 20-Year Tawny

*"This is a perfect late summer menu. The chocolate bread pudding has
been on the menu at Zenith since its inception."* —Kevin Taylor

Lamb, Lentil and Artichoke Salad with Rosemary Pepper Vinaigrette

Serves 4 to 6

Salad

8 ounces tenderloin of lamb, room temperature

1 tsp. each fresh thyme, parsley, sage and rosemary

1/2 tsp. minced fresh garlic

Small leaves of various baby lettuces, endives and greens,
    such as red romaine, red and green oak leaf, mâche,
    arugula, radicchio, Belgian endive, cress

1 cup cooked lentils

1/4 cup each finely diced fennel, tomato and shallot

1/2 cup canned baby artichokes, quartered

Bring lamb to room temperature. Mix fresh thyme, parsley, sage, rosemary and garlic together. Rub lamb with the mixture.

Broil tenderloin of lamb for 3 to 4 minutes on each side.

Arrange salad leaves on plate topping them with 1 leaf of radicchio.

Mix lentils, diced vegetables and artichokes together. Slowly warm in a steamer for a few minutes. Spoon over salad greens.

Slice lamb in thin slices and fan atop warm lentil mixture. Top with Rosemary Pepper Vinaigrette

Rosemary Pepper Vinaigrette
Makes 3/4 cup

1 Tbsp. fresh rosemary sprigs (picked clean of large stem)

1 shallot, chopped

1/2 tsp. freshly ground black pepper

3 Tbsp. lemon juice, strained

Pinch of salt

1/2 tsp brown sugar

2/3 cup good quality olive oil

4 Tbsp. balsamic vinegar

Place all the ingredients in blender. Blend at high speed until smooth.

Charbroiled Tuna with Black Bean "Chili",
Orange Crema and Mango Tomatillo Salsa

Serves 4

Black Bean "Chili"

1 1/2 cups black beans

1 Tbsp. olive oil

1 small onion, finely diced

2 serrano chilis, finely diced

1 1/2 Tbsp. cumin

1 tsp. balsamic vinegar

6 cups chicken stock (see Madeleine's Pantry)

Salt and pepper to taste

Cilantro sprigs and slices of lime, for garnish

Soak beans in water overnight. Drain.

Pour olive oil in Dutch oven or heavy saucepan. Over medium heat sauté onion, chilis and cumin, stirring until onion begins to brown. Add black beans, vinegar and chicken stock and simmer, covered, until beans are soft (about 60 to 90 minutes).

Remove 1/4 of beans and purée in blender. Add to remaining beans. Season to taste with salt and pepper. Finish cooking until beans resemble slightly thickened chili, 10 to 15 minutes longer.

Leftover "chili" may be kept in the refigerator for several days.

Orange Crema
Makes 1/2 cup

1/2 cup nonfat plain yogurt
Juice and grated zest of 2 oranges

Blend ingredients together and set aside.

Mango Tomatillo Salsa
Makes about 2 cups

1 mango, peeled and diced (papaya may be used instead)
4 small tomatillos, husked and diced
  (tomatoes may be substituted)
1/4 cup diced yellow sweet pepper
2 red serrano chilis, diced
1 Tbsp. honey
Juice of 1 lime
Salt to taste
6 tuna steaks, 3/4-inch thick

Combine all ingredients, except tuna steaks, and let set 20 minutes for flavors to blend.

Charbroil tuna steaks over hot grill for 4 to 5 minutes on each side. Do not overcook.

Presentation: Spoon Black Bean "Chili" on plate to fully cover by 1/4 inch. Place tuna on top of black beans. Spoon Mango Tomatillo Salsa on top of tuna and drizzle with Orange Crema. Garnish with cilantro sprigs and lime slices.

Serves 8 to 10

Chocolate Bread Pudding

1 French baguette

4 ounces (1 stick) unsalted butter, melted

8 ounces (1 cup) good quality semi-sweet chocolate

3 cups heavy cream

1 cup milk

2 whole eggs, room temperature

8 egg yolks, room temperature

1/2 cup sugar

1 Tbsp. vanilla extract

Grease a 9x2-inch cake pan. Cut baguette into 1/4-inch slices and brush with melted butter. Put under broiler for a few seconds, being careful not to let it burn. Set aside.

Melt chocolate in top of double boiler over simmering water. Set aside. Heat cream and milk until warm to the touch, being careful not to scald. Beat whole eggs, egg yolks, sugar and vanilla together. Slowly pour warm cream and milk over egg mixture and blend well. Pour mixture into chocolate and whisk until no lumps of sugar remain.

Line bread slices, buttered side up, into greased pan until pan is full.

Pour chocolate mixture into pan and let rest for 40 minutes or until all bread is soaked.

Preheat oven to 350°F. Bake in a water bath for 40 to 50 minutes or until knife inserted in center comes out clean. Let cool overnight.

Chocolate Sauce
Makes 1 cup

2-ounces unsweetened chocolate

1 Tbsp. butter, melted

1/3 cup boiling water

1/2 cup sugar

3 Tbsp. corn syrup

1 tsp. vanilla

Melt chocolate in top of double boiler over simmering water. Transfer to a small saucepan. Add melted butter and blend well. Add boiling water, sugar and corn syrup and stir well. Gently boil uncovered, for 3 minutes. Remove from heat and add vanilla.

When ready to serve, slightly warm bottom of cake pan and slide knife around edges. Invert bread pudding on serving platter and serve with Chocolate Sauce.

Philippe Van Cappellen
Picasso Restaurant

The Lodge at Cordillera. Located only a few minutes from Beaver Creek and surrounded by thirty-two hundred acres of pristine wilderness and towering mountains, the Lodge at Cordillera rests on a secluded perch, high in Vail Valley's New York Range. A drive through an imposing twin-pillared gate and two miles of gently winding road leads to this twenty-eight room luxurious spa resort.

Your first glance of the lodge evokes the image of a romantic European chateau in the Pyrénées country. Managing owner, Bill Clinkenbeard, commissioned Belgian architect, Léon Lambotte, to design it. He, in turn, used his adopted homeland of Northern Spain for inspiration.

The Lodge at Cordillera reflects a meticulous choice of materials. The Chinese slate roof came from the same quarry that produced the Great Wall of China. The maplewood and native stones blend the elegance of European design with the splendor of the Rocky Mountains.

Cordillera is home to Restaurant Picasso, named for the artist whose original work adorns the walls. Belgian chef, Philippe Van Cappellen, recipient of a "Diplôme d'honneur du Club des gastronomes de Belgique," reigns over the modern and superbly-equipped kitchen designed by Jacques Deluc, former executive chef of the Barbizon restaurant in Brussels.

Philippe wanted to cook ever since he was a little boy. His mother, a fine cook in her own right, recognized this and let him share in the kitchen work. Later he enrolled in the culinary school in Brussels. After graduation he wanted to learn "what the role of the chef really was." He did several "stages" or apprenticeships in restaurants and discovered that he liked both the rigorous schedule and work. These "stages" allowed him different visions of the cooking world that instilled in him a desire to explore other avenues of cuisine.

France called and he went to Troyes to be the sous-chef to Jean-Paul Duquesnoy, now the owner and executive chef of the well-known restaurant, Duquesnoy, in Paris. From there, he moved on to a summer of work for Patrick Lenôtre of the famed pastry team of Patrick and Gaston Lenôtre, who were then taking care of the Hotel Bibelot in St. Tropez. Then a friend, the chef at Chateau d'Esclémont in Chartres, offered him the job of sous-chef and he accepted. Two weeks later, his friend had to leave on an emergency and Philippe, at twenty-four years of age, became the chef of the Chateau's restaurant.

After one and a half years and more training and "stages," he was offered the position of chef at La Charlotte aux Pommes, a small, inexpensive restaurant that had just opened in Brussels. He accepted this challenge, feeling that it would be a great opportunity for him to use his expertise as a chef. He cooked both lunches and dinners and covered every facet of food preparation from bread to pastry to main courses.

The restaurant was an instant success and went on to win the Belgian "Best Restaurant of the Year" award.

This reaffirmed Philippe's strong belief in the importance of using the freshest possible ingredients and delivering them properly - a philosophy he maintains to this day.

Philippe Van Cappellen was asked to oversee the operation of Picasso at the Lodge at Cordillera two and a half years ago. In this short time, this extraordinarily talented chef has established the restaurant as one of the "merveille" of the Rockies.

A Fantasy Snowstorm Dinner Menu For Six

Salmon Wrapped in Grape Leaves with Tomato Basil Vinaigrette

Lamb Chops Filled with Foie Gras

Marquise Au Chocolat

Wine Recommendations

1989 Pinot Gris, Hugel, Alsace

1986 Chateau L'Evangile, Pomerol

Porto Warres Warrior

"During the Colorado winters, cozy nights by the fire, while the storm roars outside, can be the happiest and most inspiring of times. Nature is the ever-powerful dictator, yet we may comfort ourselves with rich and healthy food."   —*Phillipe Van Cappellan*

Salmon Wrapped in Grape Leaves with
Tomato Basil Vinaigrette

Serves 6

Salmon

6 portions of salmon fillet, 3 to 4 ounces each

Salt and pepper

12 grape leaves (available in jars at most grocery stores)

1/3 cup olive oil

Preheat broiler. Season salmon pieces with salt and pepper. Wrap each portion in two grape leaves, being sure to cover top side of fish completely. Place on a greased sheet pan and brush well with olive oil. Broil, basting occasionally for 6 minutes.

Remove grape leaves and invert salmon onto a small plate. Cover with Tomato Basil Vinaigrette.

Tomato Basil Vinaigrette

1/2 tsp. Dijon mustard

Pinch of salt

Dash of freshly ground pepper

2 Tbsp. red wine vinegar

12 Tbsp. good quality olive oil

4 tomatoes, peeled, seeded and finely diced

12 basil leaves

In a medium-size bowl, dissolve mustard, salt and pepper in vinegar. Add oil in a thin stream, mixing with a whisk to emulsify. Correct seasoning. Add tomatoes and basil. Cover and refrigerate overnight.

Serves 6

12 small lamb chops, 1 1/2-inches thick, fat removed

Salt and pepper

1 small can imported foie gras

12 pieces foil paper to wrap lamb chops

Clarified butter (see Madeleine's Pantry)

Split lamb chops horizontally to obtain two flaps of meat attached to bone. Season inside with salt and pepper. Cut foie gras into 12 equal pieces. Fill each chop with a piece of foie gras. Wrap each lamb chop, like a package, in a piece of foil paper.

Melt clarified butter in heavy large skillet, over medium-high heat. Cook lamb chops, covered, for 20 to 25 minutes, turning once. Check for doneness.

Remove foil and serve with seasonal vegetables.

Marquise Au Chocolat

Serves 12 to 14

1 porcelain terrine, 6 1/2 cups in size

17 1/2 ounces European bittersweet chocolate
    (not unsweetened)*

2 sticks plus 3 Tbsp. unsalted butter

3/4 cup plus 4 Tbsp. powdered sugar, sifted

10 egg yolks, room temperature

5 egg whites, room temperature

2 Tbsp. sugar

1 1/4 cups heavy cream, cold

*Available at specialty food stores

Line terrine with plastic wrap.

Chop chocolate into small pieces and put in top of double boiler with butter and powdered sugar, stir occasionally, until melted and smooth.

Lightly beat egg yolks for 1 minute. In another bowl, beat egg whites until stiff. Add the 2 tablespoons of sugar, beat 1 more minute. In a separate bowl, beat heavy cream until half whipped. Set ingredients aside.

When chocolate mixture is ready, transfer it to a large bowl and gently whisk in yolks. Immediately fold in egg whites, then cream, working quickly so the mixture does not stiffen.

Pour mixture into prepared terrine and refrigerate overnight.

Invert terrine on a serving platter. Remove plastic wrap. Slice and garnish each piece with fresh fruit or coulis of your choice.

This Marquise au Chocolat freezes well.

Pam Van Poollen
Transalpin

Pam Van Poollen's life over the last seven years reads like a dream play:

Act 1. Earn two degrees from the University of Hawaii, a bachelor's in psychology and a master's in exercise physiology.

Act 2. Meet husband-to-be in Hawaii, marry and move to the mainland to live in his home state of Colorado.

Act 3. Work at St. Joseph Hospital in her field of interest, cardio-vascular technology.

But soon, life was to take a dramatic turn for this young lady and enter "an entirely new play." Now settled on the mainland, Pam's thoughts drifted back to her home in Hawaii and to the many parties her Chinese mother gave. She remembered how much she had enjoyed helping her mother, especially tasting the many different foods in Hawaii. Because of the islands' location between the Orient and the West Coast of the United States, she had sampled everything from Korean, Philippine, Vietnamese, Japanese and Chinese to French and American cuisine.

Perhaps, she thought, she had selected the wrong career. Pam decided to get a part-time job as a cook. She loved the work so she resigned her position at the hospital to continue her culinary education. As Pam says,"I have come up through the ranks."

Her first full-time work in the field was as a pantry cook at La Bonne Soupe restaurant. She went on to Café Giovanni and Al Fresco. A sous-chef position at the Zenith and Pomodoro restaurants helped her acquire an excellent knowledge of Southwestern and Italian cuisine.

In January, 1991, Transalpin restaurant hired her as its chef. This dining establishment, with its eclectic cuisine, has enabled Pam to utilize her medical-educational background to implement a healthful cooking style. Her new menu avoids fats and heavy sauces and features grilled items, pastas and salads, all geared to make dining a healthy, yet pleasurable experience. "This is a fun place to be and I love my work," she says.

A Fantasy Snowstorm Dinner Menu for Six

Fishcakes with Hoisin Sauce

Chicken Curry Stirfry

Mango Sorbet

Wine Recommendation

1989 Heyl zu Herrnsheim Niersteiner Pettenthal,
Riesling, Spatlese Halbtrocken, Rheinhesse

"Hawaii is known as the melting pot of the Pacific, a place where East meets West. Having been born and raised there, I am fortunate to have been exposed to many different styles of food. These dishes typify the various combinations of ethnic cuisine there." —Pam Van Poollen

Serves 6

1 lb. white fish, cubed (orange roughy or cod)

1 lb. medium-size shrimp, peeled, deveined, cut-up

12 water chestnuts, diced

2 eggs

1/4 cup green onions, diced

1/4 cup fresh cilantro, chopped

Salt and pepper to taste

Flour

3 Tbsp. peanut oil

Hoisin sauce

    (available in Oriental section of supermarkets)

In a food processor, combine all ingredients except flour, peanut oil and Hoisin Sauce and purée for 1 minute. Transfer to a bowl, cover and chill for 1/2 hour. Take 2 tablespoons fish cake mixture and form into a ball with hands. Flatten into a patty and lightly coat with flour. Proceed with remaining mixture.

In a large heavy sauté pan over high heat, warm 3 Tbsp. peanut oil. Reduce heat to medium and fry patties until golden brown, about 3 minutes on each side. Serve with Hoisin sauce.

Chicken Curry Stirfry

Serves 6

1 lb. penne pasta

1 Tbsp. olive oil

4 Tbsp. curry oil (recipe follows)

3 chicken breast halves, deboned,
   skinned and cut into 2-inch strips

1 1/2 Tbsp. garlic, minced

1 1/2 Tbsp. ginger root, minced

1 large onion, sliced

3/4 cup carrots, thinly sliced

3/4 cup celery, thinly sliced

3/4 cup broccoli, chopped

1 red bell pepper, julienned

1 green bell pepper, julienned

1 yellow bell pepper, julienned

Salt and pepper

Dash cayenne pepper

1/2 cup green onions, finely chopped

Bring 4 quarts of water to a boil in a large pot. Stir in a teaspoon of salt. Add penne pasta and cook until tender but still firm: do not overcook. Drain pasta well and transfer to a pot. Toss with olive oil. Keep warm.

In a heavy sauté pan, over medium heat, warm 2 Tbsp. curry oil. Sauté chicken strips, stirring, for 3 minutes. Turn heat down to medium, add 2 Tbsp. curry oil and cook another 30 seconds. Add garlic, ginger root, onion, carrots, celery and broccoli. Stir well and sauté 5 more minutes. Add bell peppers and cook until heated through. Season with salt, pepper and cayenne to taste.

Presentation: Toss cooked pasta with stirfry. Divide onto 6 warm plates and garnish each with some chopped green onions. Serve at once.

Curry Oil

1/2 cup canola oil
2 1/2 tsp. curry powder

Stir to combine, let stand 20 minutes (leftover oil keeps well).

Mango Sorbet

Serves 6

4 ripe mangos
1/2 cup simple syrup (recipe follows)
5 Tbsp. fresh lemon juice
Mint sprigs, for garnish

Peel mangos, cut in halves, remove seeds, cut into cubes. Place in food processor and purée (you should have 2 cups purée). Stir simple syrup and lemon juice into purée.

Place mixture in ice-cream machine and process according to manufacturer's instructions OR

Place mixture in ice cube trays. When ready to serve, place sorbet "cubes" in food processor and purée until soft. Serve at once.

Garnish each helping of sorbet with a sprig of mint.

Simple syrup

2 cups water
3/4 cup sugar

In a small pan over medium heat, put water and sugar. Stir and bring to a boil. Reduce heat and simmer for 3 minutes. Cool. Pour into a jar, cover and refrigerate (syrup will keep for several weeks).

Executive Chef Chris Wing
The Ranch at Keystone

The prevailing atmosphere of the Ranch at Keystone is reminiscent of the rustic past and western heritage of this idyllic mountain valley. Long before the white man came to settle here, the Ute and Arapahoe Indians made this area their summer campground, hunting and fishing the woodlands, streams and meadows.

In 1938, Luke E. Smith came to this peaceful valley, bought three original homesteads and began and operated a cattle ranch until 1972.

The inside of the Ranch is as inspiring as the view outside. The large pine log walls were cut from trees of the Keystone mountain. The imposing fireplace, around which the home was built, was a wedding gift from Luke to his daughter, Bernardine, when she married Howard Reynolds in 1930. Dining at Keystone Ranch makes you feel special, as if you are dining in someone's home.

Executive Chef Chris Wing oversees the nine restaurants which comprise the Keystone Resort. He was not trained as a chef, but entered the culinary world by a different road.

It began when he was graduated in 1972 from the University of California at Berkeley with a degree in philosophy. He had many friends and associates in the academic world who were interested in fine dining. They found a predominance of French cuisine there. The chefs imported both the ideas and the food, particularly Dover sole, from Europe rather than using the abundant local produce and fish from their own ocean.

People in Berkeley were becoming excited about the culinary world. To quote Chris, "There was a buzz in the air about food," and he wanted to become a part of it. Despite his lack of formal training, he felt he could learn through working with other chefs and then develop his own style. The difference would be to use food produced and available in one's own locale and to prepare it in a classical manner.

After a brief time in California, he was offered a position in Hawaii, where he was asked to prepare food in the typical European style. He noticed that Hawaiian chefs were reluctant to utilize local ingredients even though they used them in their own homes. They believed that guests from the mainland would not be interested in this type of food. However, he gradually worked many of these foods into his menus and helped to create a "Hawaiian Cuisine" that was unique for the area.

After seven years in Hawaii, Chris returned to the mainland and came to Colorado. Today, he is exercising his unusual creativity again, giving his cuisine a "Rocky Mountain kind of feel," accommodating his menu to rustic mountain dining in a unique and splendid way.

Summer Garden Party Menu for Six

Chilled Bisque of Dungeness Crab with Rainbow Peppers

Whole Roast Garlic Eggplant Salad over Greens with Couscous,
Sherry Vinaigrette and Heart Croutons

Grilled Citrus Marinated Chicken with a Fresh Peach Salsa and
Whole Kernel Southwest-Style Polenta

Granité of Sweet Melon

Wine Recommendations

1990 Semillon, Columbia, Washington

1990 Brouilly, Georges Duboeuf

Mumm Cuvée Napa Blanc de Noir

"Summer has a cuisine all its own. It is redolent of peppers, garlic and eggplant. Foods that are grilled in the backyard, wonderfully ripe melons and pit fruits such as peaches and sweet West Coast Dungeness crab. Summer is a time for friends to gather for informal parties; and this is a menu of ingredients for a summer party."

"You will find, however, that the peach is not peeled and neither is the eggplant and the garlic isn't even minced, but served whole. Yet the tastes are full and the menu leaves time for the ones you love." —Chris Wing

Serves 6

1 Tbsp. olive oil

2 garlic cloves, peeled

1/2 cup onion, peeled, chopped

1/2 cup russet potato, peeled, chopped

1/2 cup carrot, peeled, chopped

1 cup white wine

1 can natural clam juice

1 cup water

1/2 cup heavy cream

1/2 tsp. salt

1/2 tsp. coarsely cracked white pepper

1 tsp. fresh thyme leaf

1/2 whole nutmeg, shaved or grated

1/2 Tbsp. whole grain Dijon mustard

3/4 Tbsp. Hungarian paprika

1 dash Tabasco

1/2 cup cooked Dungeness crab meat, cut up

1/2 cup red bell pepper, seeded, julienned

1/2 cup green bell pepper, seeded, julienned

1/2 cup yellow bell pepper, seeded, julienned

Heat olive oil in a large heavy pan over moderate heat. Sauté garlic and onion until soft. Add potato and carrot and cook a few more minutes. Add the white wine and simmer for 10 minutes. Add clam juice, water and cream and continue cooking until the vegetables are soft while adding salt, pepper, thyme, nutmeg, Dijon mustard, paprika and Tabasco.

Strain the solids, reserving the liquid. Purée the solids in a food processor or blender. Return the purée to the liquids. Add the crabmeat. Taste for any "raw" alcohol flavor from the wine. If it is still present, simmer until the flavor dissipates. Put the thin slivers of peppers in a storage or serving pan, pour the hot soup over and refrigerate immediately to cool the soup and retain the colors of the peppers. Serve in chilled cups.

Whole Roast Garlic Eggplant Salad over Greens with Couscous, Sherry Vinaigrette and Heart Croutons

Serves 6

Salad

1 1-lb. eggplant, cut into 3/8 inch cubes, skin on

1/4 cup salt

1 cup olive oil

1 red onion, cut into 3/8-inch cubes

1 Tbsp. minced fresh ginger

1/4 cup whole garlic cloves, roasted and peeled
(see Madeleine's Pantry)

1 red pepper, seeded, cut into 3/8-inch cubes

1 green pepper, seeded, cut into 3/8-inch cubes

1 yellow pepper, seeded, cut into 3/8-inch cubes

1 cup fresh basil, minced

1 tsp. salt

1 tsp. coarsely cracked white pepper

1 tsp. anchovy paste

1 Tbsp. whole grain Dijon mustard

2 Tbsp. capers

1/2 cup Sherry vinegar

6 heart-shaped croutons, sautéed in butter, for garnish

Cut the eggplant and toss with 1/4 cup salt. Let sit in a bowl for 1/2 hour. Rinse thoroughly with water and drain well.

Heat oil in a heavy sauté pan over moderate heat. Add diced eggplant and cook, stirring occasionally, for 3 minutes. Add onion, ginger, roasted garlic and stir, cook 1 minute. Add peppers, cook another minute. Add remaining ingredients, stir, remove from heat and cool in the refrigerator.

Couscous

1 cup whole wheat couscous

1/2 whole nutmeg, shaved or grated

1/2 tsp. salt, or to taste

1/4 tsp. cumin

2 Tbsp. unsalted butter

1/2 cup boiling water

Heat oven to 350°F.

Mix the dry ingredients together. Melt the butter in the boiling water and mix into the dry ingredients. Cover tightly and cook in oven for 20 minutes. Fluff with a fork and chill.

Sherry Vinaigrette
Makes about 2 1/4 cups

1 cup extra virgin olive oil

1 cup Sherry wine vinegar

1 tsp. ground black pepper

2 tsp. whole grain Dijon mustard

2 tsp. anchovy paste

4 Tbsp. fresh basil, minced

8 garlic cloves, minced

Mix all ingredients together and let sit for 1/2 hour at room temperature before serving.

Presentation: Have an assortment of field greens consisting of rocket, frisée, radicchio, dandelion greens, red oak lettuce and red Belgian endive. Arrange the greens on chilled salad plates. Place some couscous over the greens followed by some eggplant salad. Drizzle the vinaigrette all over and garnish with heart-shaped croutons.

Grilled Citrus Marinated Chicken with a Fresh Peach Salsa and Whole Kernel Southwest-Style Polenta

Serves 8

Grilled Citrus Marinated Chicken

8 chicken breast halves, skinned and boned

Citrus Marinade

Juice and grated zest of 1 orange, 1 grapefruit and 1 lime

1 Tbsp. fresh ginger, minced

5 garlic cloves, minced

1/4 cup olive oil

1 Tbsp. honey

1 Tbsp. whole grain Dijon mustard

1 tsp. anchovy paste

1/2 tsp. salt

1/4 tsp. pepper, or to taste

Place chicken in a Pyrex dish. Mix the citrus zest and juice with the remaining ingredients. Correct seasoning. Rub the marinade on the chicken breasts and let it sit, covered, in refrigerator for 2 hours or longer.

When ready to serve, grill chicken on an outdoor grill or under a preheated broiler for 4 to 5 minutes on each side. Serve with salsa (recipe follows) and polenta (recipe follows) and garnish with cilantro leaves.

Peach Salsa
Makes 3 cups

1 pound ripe peaches, peeled, chopped

1 Tbsp. olive oil

1 Tbsp. firm-packed cilantro, minced

2 tsp. lemon juice

1 tsp. honey

1/2 tsp. salt

1/4 tsp. ground white pepper

1 tsp. dried crushed chili peppers

1 tsp. cumin

Peel and chop peaches. Place in a bowl and mix with the remaining ingredients. Let sit in refrigerator for 1 hour.

Whole Kernel Southwest-Style Polenta

1/2 pound whole fresh Anaheim peppers

1 pound frozen whole kernel corn, defrosted

2 cups yellow cornmeal

5 cups water

1 Tbsp. honey

1 whole nutmeg, shaved or grated

1/2 bunch fresh cilantro, minced

1 tsp. ground cumin

1 Tbsp. fresh ginger, minced

1 tsp. coarsely cracked white pepper

1 tsp. salt

1/4 tsp. dry mustard

1/4 tsp. dried crushed chili peppers

6 cilantro sprigs for garnish

Preheat oven to 350°F. Roast the peppers (see Madeleine's Pantry). Peel, seed and dice. Mix the peppers with the remaining ingredients and pour into a 7 1/2 inch x 3 inch round baking dish. Bake for 1 hour, stirring once or twice the first 15 minutes.

Serves 6

2 pounds cantaloupe*

1 1/2 Tbsp. fresh ginger, minced

3 Tbsp. honey

Juice and grated zest of 1 lemon

2 Tbsp. Irish whiskey

Zest of 1 lime, for garnish.

*This recipe works well with any ripe melon, casaba,
    crenshaw or Persian

Peel cantaloupe. Seed and purée in processor or blender (you should have 6 cups cantaloupe).

Put purée in a bowl. Add remaining ingredients except lime zest and place in the freezer, stirring occasionally while it is freezing to break up the ice. The result is not a smooth sherbet, but a rustic ice. Garnish each serving with a little lime zest.

Brian Wood
Chives American Bistro

Brian Wood was twelve years old when the Culinary Institute of America moved from Connecticut to his hometown, Hyde Park, New York. For him, it was love at first sight. Brian thought how interesting and enjoyable it would be to enroll at the Institute to become a chef. Three years later, his father began working as a supervisor at the Institute, a move that would make it easier for Brian to become a student there.

He began preparing himself by working in different delis and restaurants in upstate New York and acquired a good knowledge of Italian food. He joined the Institute after high school and graduated in 1982.

After moving to Denver, Brian was hired at Dudley's, the premier French restaurant of Denver at the time. There he worked his way to the position of sous-chef and after two years was hired by Tante Louise as its sous-chef. He stayed there for another two years.

The time had come, he felt, to find a place to build his career as a chef. After a few unsuccessful tries, luck came his way. Chives American Bistro was in need of a chef and Brian was the person they wanted.

In order to increase and broaden Chives' business, Brian immediately began a catering company. The venture proved very successful, enabling the restaurant to maintain its excellent evening dining.

Chives calls itself a "new American bistro," which to Brian means, "the freedom to do what one wants with no boundaries whatsoever." He is not afraid to borrow from other cultures, and creates, for example, Oriental-style dishes using either American or Asian ingredients. He combines western-style cooking with French and Italian influences.

Brian attributes the success of the restaurant to its reasonable prices and the consistency in the quality of the food.

"Some of the benefits of being a chef are having the availability to wonderous foods, low cost ingredients and a full stomach at all times. In this day with the AIDS crisis, we, as chefs have to look beyond ourselves to the starving and disabled. We need to share the wealth with the others who, for whatever reason, cannot feed themselves."

The following menu reflects the versatility of Chives.

Menu for Six

Jalapeño Cornbread with Honey Butter

**Grilled Stuffed Chicken Breast with Prosciutto Ham and
Smoked Mozzarella, Garlic Basil Cream Sauce**

Apple Sundried Cherry Pie

Wine Recommendations

1988 Chianti Classico, Gabbiano

*1987 Johannisberg Riesling Late Harvest,
Babcock Vineyards, Santa Ynez*

"The **Friends for Dinner** *cookbook is a good example of chefs and restaurant owners who share some of the wealth. Meals on Wheels for People with AIDS is a way for us to help those who have been customers, friends and employees in the past, and for the people we know now that in the future might possibly need our help."* —Brian Wood

Jalapeño Cornbread with Honey Butter

Serves 6 to 8

3 cups cornmeal (yellow or white)
3 cups all purpose flour, sifted
1 tsp. salt
1 1/2 tsp. baking powder
6 eggs
1/2 cup honey
1 1/2 cups half and half
1 1/2 cups milk
1/2 cup buttermilk
1/4 cup plus 3 Tbsp. butter, melted
5 jalapeño peppers, seeded and diced

Preheat oven to 400°F. Generously grease a 9x13-inch pan. Set aside.

In a bowl, combine cornmeal, flour, salt and baking powder. Set aside.

In a medium bowl, lightly beat eggs. Add honey. Stir in half and half, milk, buttermilk and butter. Stir into dry ingredients and mix only until dry ingredients are moistened. Add jalapeño peppers and stir briefly. Turn into prepared pan.

Bake for 30 to 40 minutes. Do not overcook. Cool to room temperature and serve with Honey Butter.

Honey Butter
Makes 1/2 cup

1 stick (4 ounces) unsalted butter, room temperature
1/2 Tbsp. honey
1 tsp. molasses

Mix all ingredients together. Chill. Serve with Jalapeño Cornbread.

Grilled Stuffed Chicken Breast with Prosciutto Ham and Smoked Mozzarella, Garlic Basil Cream Sauce

Serves 6

Grilled Stuffed Chicken Breast

6 whole chicken breasts, deboned, skin on

6 thin slices of prosciutto ham, cut in half

12 slices of smoked mozzarella, 1/2-ounce each

Basil leaves, for garnish

Cut a pocket on each side of the chicken breasts. Place a slice of prosciutto ham around each slice of mozzarella; stuff the wrapped mozzarella in each of the pockets in the chicken.

Preheat oven to 400°F.

Grill chicken breasts on the skin side only for 4 to 5 minutes. Remove carefully and transfer to a greased 9x13-inch Pyrex dish. Continue cooking in the oven for 10 minutes more. Do not overcook.

Garlic Basil Cream Sauce
Makes 1 cup

4 cloves garlic, unpeeled

2 cups half and half

4 Tbsp. fresh basil, finely chopped

Salt and pepper to taste

Fresh basil sprigs for garnish

Heat oven to 350°F. Roast garlic for 30 minutes (see Madeleine's Pantry). Cool slightly; peel and finely chop.

In a medium saucepan, put cream and chopped roasted garlic. Reduce by half. Add basil and season with salt and pepper to taste. Set aside and keep warm.

Presentation: Pour 3 to 4 tablespoons Garlic Basil Cream Sauce on plate and place a chicken breast over sauce. Garnish with a sprig of basil.

Serves 6 to 8

Pie Shell
Makes one double crust 9-inch pie shell

2 1/2 cups all purpose flour, sifted

1/2 tsp. sugar

3/4 tsp. salt

2 sticks (8 ounces) unsalted butter, cut into pieces

1/3 cup ice cold water

Chill flour, sugar, salt and butter. Place in a food processor fitted with the metal blade and pulse 10 times or until mixture resembles small peas.

With machine on, add water in a steady stream and pulse only until dough holds together. Divide dough in half, make 2 flat disks. Wrap each in waxed paper. Chill for 30 minutes.

Filling

1 cup sundried cherries
   (available at specialty food stores)

7 Granny Smith apples, peeled, cored and thinly sliced

3/4 cup brown sugar

1 Tbsp. flour

1 Tbsp. cornstarch

1/4 tsp. cinnamon

2 Tbsp. unsalted butter, cut up

Soak sundried cherries in warm water for 5 minutes. Drain. Mix cherries, brown sugar, flour, cornstarch and cinnamon together. Set aside.

Preheat oven to 350°F.

Roll each pastry disk on a floured pastry board to an 11-inch circle.

Ease bottom crust into pie pan and leave the edge untrimmed. Put in the filling. Dot with butter pieces. Moisten edges of lower crust with water and lay top crust over filling. Cut design for steam vents. Press lower and upper crusts together. Trim both together about 1/4-inch beyond the rim of the pan. Fold the edge under and flute.

Bake for about 1 hour, 10 minutes or until done.

Beef Stock
Makes 2 1/2 quarts

Stock, broth and bouillon are interchangeable names for the same thing: the liquid obtained by cooking meat, bones and vegetables together.

3 lbs. beef bones

1 lb. veal shank

2 red onions, roughly chopped

3 large carrots, roughly chopped

2 leeks, thickly sliced

3 to 4 ribs celery, thickly sliced

1 red onion, cut in half

A few mushroom stalks or trimmings

2 to 3 soft, ripe tomatoes

1 tsp. salt

3 sprigs parsley

1 sprig thyme or a pinch of dried thyme

1 bay leaf

1 clove

9 black peppercorns

Preheat oven to 450°F.

Trim any excess fat from the meat. Put beef and veal bones in a roasting pan. Add roughly chopped onions, carrots, sliced leeks and celery. Roast for 20 to 30 minutes, turning occasionally, until richly browned.

To color stock, place the onion halves cut side down in a pan over high heat and sear until they are well browned.

Scrape contents of roasting pan into a large stock pot. Add seared onion halves, boned meat, mushrooms and tomatoes. Add 1/2 pint cold water to the roasting pan and bring it to a boil on top of the stove, scraping the bottom and the sides with a wooden spoon to dislodge all the crusty bits and sediment. Add to the stockpot. Add 5 1/2 pints cold water. Place the pot over low heat and slowly bring to a boil. Allow foam to settle into scum on the surface, skim it off with a slotted spoon. Then add salt. (Salt will draw out more scum, so, skim again.)

When all the scum has been drawn out, add parsley, thyme, bay leaf, clove and black peppercorns. Lower heat to simmer, skim again and leave to simmer very gently for 3 hours. Strain stock through a fine sieve into a large bowl and allow to cool quickly, uncovered. Cover and refrigerate ovenight and remove fat from the top of the stock.

If not using right away, store in the refrigerator for up to 5 days or freeze for up to 2 months.

Chicken Stock
Yield: 3 pints

3 1/2 to 4 lbs. chicken, cut up

6 pints water

Pinch of salt

6 peppercorns

1 chicken stock cube

2 leeks, roughly chopped

2 large carrots, roughly chopped

1 onion, quartered

2 whole cloves

2 ribs celery, roughly chopped

1 bouquet garni (parsley, a sprig of thyme and 1 bay leaf)

1 clove garlic

Put chicken in a large stockpot and cover with 6 pints of water. Add salt, peppercorns and chicken stock cube and bring slowly to the boil. Skim as necessary.

Simmer very gently uncovered for at least 1 hour, skimming the scum from the surface frequently. Add leeks, carrots, onion quarters stuck with cloves, celery, bouquet garni and garlic and continue cooking for 30 minutes longer, or until the chicken is very tender.

Remove chicken and vegetables with a slotted spoon. Set a large strainer over a bowl. Transfer the vegetables to the strainer and press them to extract all possible liquid. Discard them. Use a slotted spoon to transfer the chicken pieces to the strainer. Pick over the chicken; discard skin and bones. (The meat may be used for salad.)

Continue to cook the stock, over medium heat for 1 to 2 hours, or until the stock is reduced to 3 pints. Strain stock through a fine sieve into a shallow container and cool quickly in an ice bath or partly immersed in cold water. Cover and refrigerate overnight, then remove any fat that has congealed on top. Stock is ready to use or may be frozen for future use.

Fish Stock
Makes 3 cups

2 lbs. fish bones and trimmings, washed

4 cups water

Pinch of salt

1 red onion, chopped

1 carrot, chopped

1 rib celery, chopped

2 - 3 sprigs fresh parsley

1 sprig fresh thyme

1 bay leaf

4 mushrooms, chopped

12 white peppercorns

Thinly pared zest of 1/2 lemon

Juice of 1/2 lemon

Put fish bones and trimmings in a large pan and cover with 4 cups of cold water and a pinch of salt. Bring to a boil. Allow scum to settle on the surface, then skim off carefully with a spoon.

Add roughly chopped vegetables and all other ingredients and simmer uncovered, for 45 minutes. Strain through a cheesecloth-lined strainer. Cool to room temperature, uncovered, then cover and refrigerate or freeze

Veal Stock
Yield: 2 quarts

5 lbs. veal bones, cut into 2 inch pieces*

1 large carrot, peeled and cut into chunks

1 large onion, chopped

1 1/2 gallons water

1 rib celery, cut into chunks

2 garlic cloves

1 Tbsp. white peppercorns

2 bay leaves

1 Tbsp. fresh thyme leaves or 1 1/2 tsp. dried

3 Tbsp. tomato purée

1 cup dry white wine

*Rib ends from breastof veal or meaty knuckle bones make
    delicious stock.

Preheat oven to 375°F. Spread the veal bones in a shallow baking pan and bake for 10 minutes. Add the carrot, onion and celery and continue baking for 10 minutes or until bones and vegetables are golden brown.

Put the bones and vegetables in an 8 quart stock pot and add all the remaining ingredients. Pour 1 cup of water in the roasting pan and, with a wooden spoon, stir all the browned bits of meat and vegetables, then put this deglazing liquid into the stockpot. Bring the stock to a boil over high heat, skimming often as scum and fat rise to the surface. (Veal releases a lot of scum.) Reduce the heat so that the liquid barely simmers and cook, uncovered, for 6 hours, skimming as necessary.

Strain into a shallow container and cool quickly, uncovered, in an ice bath or partly immersed in cold water. Cover and chill the stock overnight in the refrigerator, then remove any fat that has congealed at the top. The stock is ready to be used or it may be frozen for up to two months.

How to Clarify Butter

Unsalted butter, cut into 1 inch pieces

Melt the butter in a heavy saucepan over low heat. Remove the pan from the heat; let the butter stand for 3 minutes and skim the froth. Strain the butter through a sieve lined with a double thickness of rinsed and squeezed cheesecloth into a bowl, leaving the milky solids in the bottom of the pan. Pour the clarified butter into a jar or crock and store it, covered, in the refrigerator. The butter keeps, covered and chilled, indefinitely.

When clarified, butter loses about one fourth of its original volume.

How to Cook Lentils
Yield: 1 1/2 cups

Place 1/2 cup uncooked lentils in a bowl; cover with water to a depth of one inch above the lentils. Allow to soak for 1 hour. Drain. Rinse twice.

Put lentils in a heavy saucepan with 3 cups water. Cover and cook over medium heat for 30 to 40 minutes or until tender.

How to Broil Oysters

Preheat Broiler. Use a baking dish and rock salt or crumpled foil to line it and hold the oysters in place.

Open the oysters, keeping meat and juices in curved half of the shell; arrange on the foil in the baking dish (or on rock salt) bedding them solidly to prevent tipping.

Set under moderately hot broiler for 2 to 3 minutes, watching carefully. Serve immediately.

How to Cook Mussels

Wash mussels thoroughly in running water until all signs of mud are gone. Now remove the byssus threads or beard. With scissors, cut the byssus threads off as close to the shell as possible. Put cleaned mussels in a heavy pan, pot, or kettle on the stove. Add half a cup of water or white wine. Cover the pot and let steam 5 to 7 minutes at high heat, until the shells are open wide and the meats are just firming and becoming loose from the shells. (Discard any mussels which did not open.) Remove the mussels from the broth, and when cool, remove the meats from the shells.

How to Roast Bell Peppers

Char the peppers either on top of the stove or under the broiler. Leave peppers in contact with a flame or heat only until skin is blackened, turning them often so they do not overcook. Transfer them to a plastic bag, twist it closed and let them stand for ten minutes. Remove blackened skins with the back of a small knife. If necessary, rinse peppers under cold running water to remove any bits of skin that remain.

Remove seeds and veins.

How to Roast Garlic

Place garlic on cookie sheet and roast for 30 minutes in a 350°F oven.

How to Toast Almonds

Toast blanched almonds in one layer on a cookie shet in a preheated 250° oven for 15 minutes.

How to Toast Hazelnuts

Toast the hazelnuts in one layer in a baking pan in a preheated 350°F oven for 10 to 15 minutes or until they are colored lightly and the skins blister. Wrap the nuts in a kitchen towel and let them steam for 1 minute. Rub the nuts in the towel to remove as much of the skin as possible and let them cool.

How to Use Phyllo Pastry Dough

If frozen, thaw overnight in refrigerator. Unroll dough. Place a damp towel on counter. Lay a sheet of waxed paper over it. Lay the stack of phyllo pastry sheets on waxed paper. Place another sheet of waxed paper over phyllo and cover with a damp towel. Remove one sheet of phyllo dough at a time, keeping remaining dough covered. (Unused dough may be repackaged and frozen.)

Pate Sucrée
Makes 1 9-inch pie crust

1 2/3 cups all-purpose flour

2 Tbsp. sugar

Pinch of salt

1 stick cold butter, cut into bits

1 large egg yolk beaten with 3 Tbsp. ice water

Stir the flour, sugar and salt together in a bowl. Add the butter and blend the mixture until it resembles coarse meal. Add yolk mixture, toss the mixture until the liquid is incorporated and form the dough into a ball. Dust it with flour and chill it in plastic wrap for 1/2 hour.

Proceed according to recipe.

This dough will keep for 3 or 4 days in the refrigerator. It may be kept a few weeks in the freezer.

Pie Shell
Makes 2 9-inch pastry shells

2 1/2 cups all-purpose flour, sifted
1/2 tsp. sugar
3/4 tsp. salt
2 sticks (8 ounces) unsalted butter, cut into pieces
1/3 cup ice cold water

Chill flour, sugar, salt and butter. Place in food processor fitted with the metal blade and pulse 10 times or until mixture resembles small peas.

With machine on, add water in a steady stream and pulse only until dough holds together. Divide dough in half. Make 2 flat disks. Wrap each in waxed paper. Chill for 30 minutes.

Roll each disk on a floured pastry board to an 11-inch circle.

Proceed with filling according to recipe.

Apricot Glaze

1 cup apricot jam
1 Tbsp. water

Put apricot jam and water in a small saucepan. Bring to a bare simmer and then strain.

Appetizers & First Courses

Broiled Oysters Provencal   72
Crostini with Ricotta and Sausage Topping   93
Eggplant Caponata   84
Feuilleté of Salmon   34
Fishcakes with Hoisin Sauce   232
Flan of Lobster and Scallops with Two Caviars   160
Flan of Scallops and Corn with Curry Sauce
    and Poblano Peppers   152
Imported Prosciutto Ham with Fresh Figs and Raspberries   73
Lobster Cake with Tomato-Chive Butter Sauce   50
Salmon Tartar   100
Salmon Wrapped in Grape Leaves with
    Tomato-Basil Vinaigrette   226
Sliced Melons   128
Summer Gazpacho with Avocado and Grilled Shrimp   170
Wild Rice Waffle with Wild Mushroom Ragout   24

Breads

Chocolate Biscuits   123
Crostini with Ricotta and Sausage Topping   93
Jalapeño Corn Fritters   171
Jalapeño Cornbread with Honey Butter   252
Moroccan Flat Bread (Ajina)   20
Onion Biscuits   173

Desserts

Apple Sundried Cherry Pie   256
Apricot Glaze   267
Blueberry Sorbet   147
Cantaloupe with Minted Yogurt Sauce   174

Fish and Seafood

*Smoked Rainbow Trout, Apple and Pistachio Salad with
    Lemon Mint Viniagrette   42*
Summer Gazpacho with Avocado and Grilled Shrimp   170

Meats

Beef Tongue with Chanterelle Mushrooms   101
*Colorado Tenderloin of Lamb with Garlic Parsley Pesto and Wild
    Mushroom Cabernet Sauce   74*
Crostini with Ricotta and Sausage Topping   93
Fennel Sausage   201
*Grilled Lamb with Mango Salad and Ginger
    Jalapeño Vinaigrette   26*
Lamb Chops filled with Foie Gras   227
*Lamb, Lentil and Artichoke Salad with Rosemary
    Pepper Vinaigrette   216*
Lamb Shanks with Garlic Mashed Potatoes   52
*Malfatti Ricotta Spinach Dumplings with Fennel
    Sausage and Sage Cream   200*
Medallions of Veal en Croûte, Sauce Diable   154
*Medallions of Venison with Pear, Lingonberry,
    Apple Chutney   12*
Tenderloin of Beef with Sauce Poivrade   187
Tenderloin of Lamb with Sweet Peppers en Strudel   163
Wild Rice Meatloaf   119

Pasta

Chicken Curry Stirfry   233
Penne Bagutta with Tomato Sauce   64
*Sautéed Lobster with Tarragon Champagne Beurre
    Blanc and Herbed Fettucini   136*
Seafood Ragout and Scallion Mornay Sauce   111

Poultry

Baked Chicken Breast with Forest Mushrooms   36
Chicken Curry Stirfry   233
Chicken Saffron   179
Dove Breast with Polenta and Kalamata Olive Sauce   129
Grilled Citrus Marinated Chicken with a Fresh
*   Peach Salsa and Whole Kernel Southwest-Style Polenta   244*
Grilled Stuffed Chicken Breast with Prosciutto
*   Ham and Smoked Mozzarella, Garlic Basil Cream Sauce   254*
Moroccan Chicken Stew   18
Penne Bagutta with Tomato Sauce   64

Salad Dressings

Basil Cumin Dressing   10
Basil Viniagrette   94
Champagne Vinaigrette   66
French Dressing   191
Ginger Jalapeño Vinaigrette   27
Green Peppercorn Lemon Vinaigrette   134
Herb Balsamic Vinaigrette   110
Lemon Mint Vinaigrette   42
Orange Vinaigrette   63
Pepper Parmesan Dressing   118
Raspberry Fig Vinaigrette   80
Rosemary Pepper Vinaigrette   217
Sauce Vinaigrette   143
Sherry Vinaigrette   243
Tomato Basil Vinaigrette   226

Salads

Arugula and Radicchio Salad 92

Charbroiled Eggplant and Champagne Vinaigrette 66

Coho Salmon, Baby Mâche and Radicchio Salad with
Orange Vinaigrette 63

Grilled Lamb with Mango Salad and Ginger
Jalapeño Vinaigrette 26

Grilled Shrimp with Roasted Tri-Color Peppers
and Basil Vinaigrette 94

Grilled Vegetable Salad with Sundried Tomato
and Herb Balsamic Vinaigrette 110

Imported Prosciutto and Fresh Figs with Raspberries 73

Lamb, Lentil and Artichoke Salad with Rosemary
Pepper Vinaigrette 216

Mango Salad 26

Mixed Green Salad with French Dressing 191

Mixed Green Salad with Pepper Parmesan Dressing 118

Roasted Pepper and Tomato Salad 19

Romaine, Radicchio and Watercress Salad with
Raspberry Fig Vinaigrette 80

Salad Shiraz 178

Shrimp with Two Melon Salad, Green Peppercorn
Lemon Vinaigrette 134

Sliced Melons 128

Sliced Tomato Salad 143

Smoked Rainbow Trout, Apple and Pistachio Salad
with Lemon Mint Vinaigrette 42

Sweet Corn, Black Bean and Artichoke Heart Salad with
Basil Cumin Dressing 10

Tomato Salad 128

Whole Roast Garlic Eggplant Salad over Greens with Couscous,
Sherry Vinaigrette and Heart Croutons 242

Sauces Savory & Sweet

Apple Grappa Cream   199
Black Bean Sauce   81
Brown Sauce   189
Chocolate Sauce   221
Citrus Marinade   244
Crème Anglaise   38
Curry Oil   234
Curry Sauce and Poblano Peppers   153
Garlic Basil Cream Sauce   255
Garlic Parsley Pesto   74
Grand Marnier Vanilla Sauce   211
Honey Butter   253
Kalamata Olive Sauce   130
Mango Tomatillo Salsa   219
Orange Crema   219
Peach Salsa   245
Pear, Lingonberry, Apple Chutney   12
Red Pepper Nage   161
Roasted Onion Mushroom Gravy   121
Roasted Red Pepper Jalapeño Rouille   83
Sage Cream   200
Sauce Diable   155
Sauce Poivrade   188
Scallion Mornay Sauce   111
Simple Syrup   235
Stilton Sabayon   156
Sweet Soy and Ginger Butter Sauce   172
Tomato Mint Chutney   44
Tomato Sauce   65, 202
Tomato-Chive Butter Sauce   51
Wild Mushroom Cabernet Sauce   75
Wild Mushroom Ragout   25

Soups

Beef Stock   259
Black Bean "Chili"   218
Chestnut Soup with Apple Grappa Cream   198
Chicken Stock   260
Chilled Bisque of Dungeness Crab with Rainbow Peppers   240
Chilled Russian Ice House Soup "Stolichnaya"   108
Chilled Strawberry Sorrel Soup   208
Fish Stock   261
Summer Gazpacho with Avocado and Grilled Shrimp   170
Veal Stock   262
Vichyssoise (Chilled Leek-Potato Soup)   142
Wild Mushroom Consommé   186

Vegetables and Starches

Asparagus Steamed with Lillet   138
Baked Spaghetti Squash with Eggplant Caponata   84
Bell Peppers, How to Roast   265
Black Bean "Chili"   218
Broccoli Florets   85
Buttermilk Mashed Potatoes   120
Charbroiled Eggplant with Champagne Vinaigrette   66
Couscous   243
Duxelles   154
Fresh Leaf Spinach   145
Garlic Mashed Potatoes   53
Garlic, How to Roast   265
Grilled Vegetable Salad with Sundried Tomato,
    Herb Balsamic Vinaigrette   110
Jalapeño Corn Fritters   171
Julienne of Carrots   190

Madeleine's Pantry